The Continuing Ripples of Living Beyond Suicide

by
Kaylene Donohue

Strategic Book Publishing and Rights Co.

Strategic Book Publishing and Rights Co.
12620 FM 1960, Suite A4-507
Houston TX 77065
www.sbpra.com

ISBN: 978-1-62212-355-1

Dedication

I would like to dedicate this book to those people we've lost to suicide, and especially to those folks who are now living beyond suicide. A very special thank you goes out to those who have been brave enough to share their stories with the hopes of helping other survivors get through the pain they've had to endure.

I would also like to thank Janine and Ron, who still allow us to have our *Living beyond Suicide* support group meetings in their home, making everybody always feel so welcome. Even after someone new finds the courage to attend a meeting for the first time, that person immediately feels comfortable, realizing that he or she is not among strangers. We will forever be linked by the same trauma: *suicide.*

A special thanks to Myrna, who willingly gives up her free time every month to act as our meeting facilitator. Myrna is a professional counselor and helps many of us try and cope with the trauma of what has happened in our lives. She is beyond patient, and even offers more of her time before and after our meetings if ever somebody needs it.

A special thanks also to the Standby team, and to Sue, who is a part of United Synergies – Noosa. Without their gracious support, we would not be able to hold our support group meetings where we do. Furthermore, there would be many people trying to cope with their grief without the assistance of our group.

There are so many special people who have touched my life in different ways, including my husband, John, who is always there for me, and my close family and friends, who have encouraged me to complete this book. Thanks so much to you all.

Contents

Note to the Reader 7

Introduction 9

1. Harley 11

2. Dianna 22

3. Barbara's Plea 31

4. Ken 33

5. Sammy's Story 39

6. Cassie's Story 43

7. Adam 47

8. Anna 50

9. Seeking Help 59

10. Support and Awareness 62

11. The Continuing Ripples 65

12. Where Are They Now? 77

Note to the Reader

After the publication of *The Healing Beach,* a book about the tragic loss of Kaylene Donohue's three children, Kaylene decided there was a definite need for more stories to be told about dealing with the crippling aftermath of suicide. As she attempted to cope with her own experiences, she realized that *many* families have had to go through the trauma of living beyond suicide—and unfortunately, there will always be more.

The Continuing Ripples of Living Beyond Suicide is inspired by true stories; however, some people's names have been changed to protect their identities. This book also touches briefly on Kaylene's life since the release of *The Healing Beach.* Hopefully, it will help bring some closure to those who are still devastated and confused by what they've had to endure. Furthermore, if you or someone you know may be contemplating suicide, this book will help you realize that there are so many ways to get help right now.

Introduction

Over the last decade, my world has been a journey of lost dreams and tragedies that I would never have believed could happen to me. Sometimes I lay awake at night and wonder just where my life is going, and then I remember how many others are in this same situation.

Suicide touched my life for the first time after the loss of my cousin. A few years later, my youngest brother took his life. While my brother's death affected me deeply, having my only three children also commit suicide has been the most devastating tragedy to try and overcome. The continuing ripple from their deaths is never-ending.

Through attending support groups and working with Head High, an organization aimed to avert youth suicide through supporting young people affected by the impacts of suicide, I have come in contact with many people from all different walks of life. The common thread joining all of us together is that we've all lost loved ones to suicide. Unfortunately, there are always so many unanswered questions, and the lack of literature there is to read about what happened to our loved ones—and *why*—only leads to more questions. How does one move on from something that is impossible to understand? How do those caught in the rippling effects of suicide survive?

Trying to find those many unanswered questions is exhausting. *Was there any warning?* That is usually one of the first questions asked. *Why? Why did they do it?* That is possibly the one question that never gets answered—at least not by most—because it's too late at that point. It could have just happened out of the blue. Either way, you feel like you should have known and been able to prevent this from happening. As your mind spins, you continue to ask yourself questions, eventually creating a pattern where you never really get anywhere, except for more lost and more confused. *Why? What could I have done differently?*

The sense of loneliness when a loved one commits suicide is incredibly overwhelming. My heart goes out to anyone who is not fortunate enough to have the ongoing support of family and friends during after such a difficult experience. I guess this is why I am now such a firm believer in support groups—both for adults as well as young people. We all need a safe place where we can discuss our feelings and not be criticized for the way we feel. It is amazing how many different stages of grief you will feel (if you aren't feeling one of them already) and the many times where you second-guess yourself as to the kind of person you are for feeling the way you do. A strong support system is key to overcoming all of this.

Personally, the overwhelming need for me to know others who have had their lives turned upside-down because of suicide—and the strong desire to listen to their stories—does not stem from a morbid sense of curiosity. It comes from an aching need inside my heart to try and find some answers, and hopefully help prevent others from taking their lives.

Suicide is a subject that no one wants to know about—at least not unless you have been touched by it yourself. The stigma of suicide is still so poignant that I have heard some families would rather say their loved one died in some other tragic way than admit to the fact that the person they loved so much had taken his or her own life. After telling my own story in *The Healing Beach,* I now find the need to speak for others in telling their stories, too, especially those who struggle with putting their emotions into words. I sincerely hope that this book helps those who are currently hurting, and desperately seeking answers and a little solace.

1. Harley

As we sat at the table with a cup of hot coffee in front of each of us, Janine slowly began telling me her story. Having heard most of it before, I knew how painful recalling the memories would be for my friend. However, she knew that sharing her story could help others dealing with the same sort of grief she had experienced; for that reason alone, she was willing to tell it again and again.

Janine and her husband, Ron, are lucky as far as marriages go. In a world full of second and third marriages, they found each other the first time around. Shortly after they got married, they decided to start a family. It didn't take long before they were overjoyed by the birth of their beautiful healthy baby girl, whom they named Renée. With a huge extended family on both sides, Janine and her husband thought their lives were full and happy. However, when Janine found out she was expecting a second child, it seemed as if life could not get any better for the young family. Life was complete, or so they believed.

Even though years had gone by, the sadness in my friend's voice was still there as she remembered the past. The pain in her eyes was still very evident. Still, she smiled at me and took a deep breath before continuing her story.

The pregnancy had proceeded without any problems, and for nine months, the baby growing inside Janine's womb was a very big part of her family's lives. She and her husband happily planned for the birth, and even picked out boy names and girl names. So when the baby was stillborn, the loss was traumatic for everyone, especially Janine.

Janine was advised by her doctor not to try and have another baby straight away. Two years later, she and her husband decided to try again for a little brother or sister for their young daughter. This time—even with everything going well—Janine's doctor did not want to take any chances. The child would be brought into the world by Cesarean section.

And so it was, Harley came into the world with all ten fingers and toes. He was a big, healthy baby, and he let everyone know he had arrived with loud cries. Once he was safely in Janine's arms, she and Ron felt their family was complete. However, even though this little baby helped to fill a void in their lives, the baby who had been lost was never forgotten.

Over the years, Harley grew into a normal, healthy young boy with fair hair and hazel eyes, just like his mother. His solid little body made him look a little older than his real age, and he could be rebellious at times, which sometimes landed him in trouble. In fact, he became quite the handful for his parents and his older sister, but he was a growing boy, and his behavior was expected.

Harley appeared to have it all. He had both parents and an older sister who loved him. He also had a large extended family. He grew up in a loving family unit where his parents were still married. Never once did they make him feel like a replacement child for their stillborn child, either. His parents were not perfect, and never pretended to be, but they were happy and did not expect too much from either of their two children. So what went wrong?

As Janine continued talking about her son, remembering the bittersweet memories of times gone by, she sometimes smiled and occasionally shed a few tears. Still, she continued to speak, telling me how she remembered her son had always gotten along with younger children. In fact, he'd even defend some of them against bullying. Harley was a hero in their young eyes, even if he *was* becoming rather unpopular with some of his teachers.

In elementary school and most of his middle school years, Harley never had any problems. He loved school and his grades were good. He also started playing football and made lots of friends. For the most part, life for Harley was happy and carefree—that is, until he reached seventh grade.

Seventh grade was the start of a troubled journey for the young boy, and that's when Janine and Ron really started seeing their son start to go downhill. It all began with one particular teacher, a woman who, according to Janine, used to pick on little kids. Harley was not a small child, so he was not one of the unfortunate students. However, one day his teacher was giving one of the smaller kids a hard time. It bothered Harley so much that he stood up to defend the child, as he often did when little kids were getting bullied. Apparently, the teacher didn't appreciate Harley stepping in, and she completely freaked out on him in front of the whole classroom. The impact that teacher had on Harley in that moment became instrumental in his behavior and trust over the ongoing years, especially with people in positions of authority.

The four years of high school are considered the most important years in education for any young student. At the same time, pressures become more demanding as students' journeys start to lead them down the path into the world of adulthood. Janine and Ron would always know from the end of the first week of the first term as to whether it would be a good year or a bad one for the whole family. The deciding factor would be the teacher Harley would be assigned to during the months to come. Unfortunately, there were some teaches at the high school whom Harley did clash with. His parents believe it was due to how Harley had been treated by the teacher who had embarrassed Harley when he was in seventh grade. Regardless of a few issues here and there, Harley excelled with his grades, and the majority of his teachers always said he was an excellent student. He was very popular among his peers, and stayed good friends with many of them throughout his young life.

When Harley reached his senior year of high school, his peers voted for him to be class president of the school. Unfortunately, he was prevented from taking up the position because he had clashed with another teacher. The extreme disappointment of losing the title just because of a teacher not liking him just caused further distress and dissolution toward those of authority. Harley was a young man who had set high goals for himself. When he wasn't able to accomplish something he set his mind to, he would then think he was a failure, not only in his own eyes but in the eyes of everyone else, too.

It was in high school that Harley realized what he wanted to do with his life. He had started to play rugby football, and as the years went by, so did his love for the sport. Harley began focusing on playing Rugby League, and he put all of his time and energy into becoming the best athlete he could be. He didn't want to do anything else except for be an amazing footballer; he wanted to make a career out of it.

As Harley matured, he turned into an outgoing young man who was full of energy. When he wasn't playing footy, he'd go fishing or crabbing with his dog, Sugar. They would often take the boat out on a weekend or holiday and bring home lots of fresh fish to have with tea. Harley was also fortunate to have come from a functional family where both parents were able to participate in their children's interests. Janine and Ron encouraged him to do the activities he enjoyed.

Harley continued to do well at football, and his future in the sport was looking bright. But the same could not be said for his schooling. He was having constant battles with his teachers, and the lack of respect he appeared to have for them reflected in his grades. Harley's education definitely began to suffer. In fact, one of the school's vice principals took an instant dislike to Harley, according to Janine, and even told him that he was nothing but a dumb footballer who would never amount to anything in life.

As I listened to my friend continue talking about her son, telling me about all the problems he had with his teachers, I realized just how much of an impact teachers really *do* make in our children's lives. Yes, a big part of the way our children are molded does come from the home that they grow up in, and how parents bring them up; however, they also spend a lot of their growing years at school. They are definitely influenced by these adults. When that trust is abused, how are these kids suppose to respect them? I didn't hesitate to believe that it was unfortunate for Janine and Ron's son to have the teachers in his life that he did. They made so much of difference in Harley's journey.

At sixteen, Harley's life took a drastic turn for the worse. One day, while playing football with his team, he took a bad fall that damaged the anterior cruciate ligament in his right knee. Surgery was needed to fix it. Although the operation was a success, and a full recovery was expected, it was this particular accident that changed Harley's life forever.

The twelve months following his operation, Harley was required to go through a lot of physiotherapy before he could start training again. It was a long and painful year as Harley tried to get his knee fit again, and a lot of hard work was needed before he could play his beloved sport once more. However, the future still looked promising, and that was all that Harley cared about. Finally, the time came when his leg was doing so well that he was able to join his teammates back on the field again. Life was wonderful, and everything seemed to quickly get back on track. In fact, Harley's game was going so well that it was now time for him to get serious if he wanted to make a career for himself.

Harley was picked to join a team to play at a carnival in Townsville, Queensland, and he was on cloud nine when he left to go on the trip with his team. If only things could have stayed that way for him—at least for a little while—but they didn't. During the very first game, his knee injury came back to haunt him. This time, though, Harley didn't need surgery. The damage wasn't as bad as it had been previously. But after that close call, knowing that the possibility of his knee injury causing further problems was suddenly foremost in Harley's mind. He was unable to get past the fact that the possibility of continuing to live his dream might not happen because his injury could stop him at any time from achieving his goals.

Harley felt in his heart that it was the end of football—and the end of his dream. It was after that realization that the light went out in his eyes. Soon after, Janine and Ron noticed their son was starting to wander around aimlessly, totally lost. Without football, Harley thought he was a failure. Furthermore, nothing seemed to make sense in his life anymore He was unable to come to terms with the traumatic change that life had dealt him and could no longer find interest in doing anything else. Harley's parents knew their son was hurting. They wanted so much to help ease his pain but just didn't know how. Nothing they tried worked.

Not caring what he did to earn some money, Harley found a job planting trees. However, when his parents learned he was being paid very little money for his work, and he was barely able to survive on his meager income, they went and immediately brought him home. Harley then enrolled at Technical and Further Education (TAFE) and also went to work for his uncle, who was a plumber. It was by no means the career choice Harley had wanted; yet it was a start. At least it would be a trade for him to get started in.

During the following months, Janine and Ron's desperation to guide their son away from the troubled path he had started to take only seemed to make the gap in their relationship with Harley wider. It became a battle to get him to go to work or to TAFE. In fact, it was a battle most mornings just to get Harley out of bed. It was like the life had already gone from him. There was just nothing the young man was interested in anymore.

At TAFE, there was one teacher who had a reputation for picking on new apprentices. Harley, with his quick temper, was the perfect candidate to be the teacher's target. Soon, it was like high school all over again for Harley. Eventually, he hated going to TAFE. After leaving the campus one particularly tough day, Harley felt so lost that he attempted to take his life. Unfortunately, Harley's parents did not find out about the bullying teacher at TAFE, or how Harley was feeling about everything, until it was much too late. Only later, after reading some of his books, did they realize how much he hated the world he lived in and how very useless he felt. Those words tore at their hearts.

Harley was no different from any other young man in terms of wanting to have a good time. While he was battling with feelings of depression, he still occasionally went to parties with his friends. One night, after drinking a little too much, he went home with a young girl he had known briefly. After that evening, he continued on with his life, never giving their sexual encounter another thought. Ten months later, however, the young girl contacted Harley with some startling news: He was the father of a one-month-old baby boy.

Naturally, Harley was shocked by the information. He hadn't seen or heard from the young mother since their one-night stand. He had no idea that she had been pregnant, and he wasn't entirely sure that the baby was his. After he told his parents, Janine and Ron felt that if their son was old enough to play grown-up games, then he was old enough to be responsible to pay for a DNA test, which was needed to determine for sure that Harley was indeed the baby's father. Janine and Ron did not want to meet the baby and form a relationship with him until they knew for certain that he was their grandson. Needless to say, it was a time of confusion for everyone involved.

Seven months later, after Harley had saved enough of his own money to pay for the DNA test—and after there had been a mix-up at the lab—he found out that he had indeed fathered the baby. The realization hit Harley—*hard.* It was not that he would not love his child; it was just not the way he had imagined having a child. Harley had wanted to fall in love first, then get married, and then have children. Suddenly, he felt as if he had not only let himself down, but he had let his parents and everyone else down as well.

Harley's self-esteem was at an all-time low. His dream career was out of the question, and he was now a father at the age of nineteen to a son conceived with a young woman he hardly knew and didn't love. With his life now completely chaotic, all he could focus on was that he was no good. It didn't matter to Harley that these kinds of things happen all the time; he expected more of himself. He couldn't stop thinking about how he had let his family down.

There were a lot of changes in that same year for Harley. Unfortunately, his beloved grandfather suddenly became ill and passed away. His relationship with his maternal grandfather had always been a close one. In fact, when his grandfather could no longer drive, Harley bought his grandfather's four-wheel drive from him so that he could drive it up the beach and spend time with his ailing grandfather. The two of them had spent time together regularly, and Harley's grandfather's death deeply affected the young man.

Even though it was a sad time for the family, at least they all knew that the grandfather had been very much loved. He had lived a long and fulfilling life. Around that same time, however, Harley was once again traumatized by death. This time a young girl he had gone to school with had suddenly and tragically taken her life.

Janine paused a moment before continuing her story, remembering the unexpected death of the young girl and how it had affected her son. Tears welled up in her eyes and began to spill down her cheeks. She quickly wiped them away and took a deep breath. When she felt composed enough to continue, she spoke quietly as I listened.

One particularly hot January day, shortly after the young girl had been buried, Janine and Harley went to the girl's gravesite to pay their respects again. The grave was still covered in a mass of flowers, and Janine thought it was depressing to know that they wouldn't last long because of the long hot summer days ahead. She and her son stood and talked of the terrible

16

loss of the girl, and it was also there that Janine made Harley swear to her that he would never take his own life. Unfortunately, it was a promise he could not keep.

Over the years, Harley had always seemed to have an unnatural curiosity about death. He was especially curious about the child whom his parents had lost so many years before. Not wanting their two children to grow up thinking death was something to be afraid of, Janine and Ron always made sure to talk openly and positively about their lost child. They often spoke of angels and of heaven being a beautiful place.

The stress over the next few months began to take its toll. According to Janine, her body was so taut with apprehension that she began to feel as if her chest would explode at any given moment. Her husband felt the same way. They both had sinking gut feelings—for weeks—that something bad would inevitably happen with their son. They just weren't sure when or what it would be.

On the Thursday before Harley's death, Janine went into Harley's room to say goodbye before she left the house. Strangely, Harley was still in bed. She tried to get her son out of bed so that he would start getting ready for work, but that only led to a heated argument between the two of them. Eventually, Janine just left, frustrated. The next day, Harley ended up going away for the weekend with his friends. He had left while still being on bad terms with his mother.

Meanwhile, Janine had decided to go and spend the weekend with her mother and her sister. It had only been a few months since the death of her father, and she felt that they needed to be there for each other in their time of grief. Janine left home that morning, her heart heavy, not knowing what else she and her husband could do to make things right for Harley. His life was going nowhere, and no matter how his family tried to help him, it only appeared to make things worse. They were at a total loss with nowhere else to turn.

While Janine stayed with her mother and sister until Monday, Harley went back home on Sunday. In hindsight, Janine believes that Harley went away with his friends that weekend to say his goodbyes to them. On Monday morning, Harley got out of bed and started getting ready for work. Then he sat down at the kitchen table to eat his breakfast. Everything seemed normal.

Ron was also in the kitchen at the time, and he remembers well how the radio had been turned on with the latest newscast just breaking. He and Harley listened intently to the horrific news of five young men, traveling home from a small country town near Wagga Wagga, New South Whales, after participating in a football match, had collided with a train at a railway crossing. Sadly, everyone in the vehicle had been killed. Once the broadcast was over, Ron remembers talking to his son about the young footballers, feeling saddened for their families and friends. However, Ron had no way of knowing that by the end of that day, he would also have lost his only son. His family's lives were about to change forever.

After breakfast and the depressing conversation, Harley left the house to go to work. Once he got there, however, he sat down at his desk and put his face in his hands. His uncle, Ron's brother, saw Harley in his unusual state and decided to call Ron immediately. After receiving his brother's worried phone call, Ron said he would just finish a small job he was working on and go pick up his son. Unfortunately, Harley did not stay and wait for his father to get there. Instead, he walked out of the workshop and drove off in his vehicle.

Ron had no idea where his son would go. As panic began to set in, he decided to call Janine and let her know what had happened; he figured she could come home and help look for their son. Strangely, though, Janine had been having a bad feeling and was already on her way from Brisbane. As soon as they hung up the phone with each other, they began making many calls to all of Harley's friends, only to come up empty-handed. Harley's sister, Renee, and other family members also quickly joined in the search. Still, Harley was nowhere to be found. All the family could do was wait and worry.

When the police eventually drove up into the driveway of their home, Janine and Ron knew something bad had happened to their son. With a sinking feeling and heavy hearts, they linked their hands together for support and headed outside to meet the officers, bracing themselves for whatever the officers had to say. Moments later, Janine and Ron were given the traumatic news.

Harley had apparently driven into a forest, believing he was a total failure and that there was no way he could get his life back on track. With that, he decided to take his life. A young boy who had been trail-riding on his bike found Harley's body hanging from a tree. Harley's car was parked nearby; a photograph of his young son photo was left sitting on the front dash. It was the last thing he would have seen before leaving the vehicle.

Janine and Ron's only son was gone just like that. The horrific nightmare for the family had suddenly begun. They desperately tried to grasp the fact that the son they had loved so much had taken his own life, but it was incomprehensible. Only more questions filled their minds. It was just so painfully hard to try and understand any of what had happened. *Why?* There had never been a suicide in their family before, so nobody really knew how to help. Fortunately, however, Janine and Ron's extended family was a large and close-knit bunch. The grieving parents and their daughter were instantly surrounded with love and support.

Harley had a lot of friends, and his death affected many young people as the news got out about what had happened. At Harley's funeral, the amount of family and friends who attended was a tribute to him. If only he had realized how many people truly cared about him, and that he would be badly missed. Didn't he know how empty his parents' and his sister's lives would be without him? What about his young son who would grow up without ever knowing his dad? Harley's actions left so many unanswered questions!

The following months for Janine and Ron were lost in a fog of confusion and pain. They desperately tried finding answers. It was only after their son's life was lost that some people began to come forward with the news that Harley had made prior attempts to take his life. However, he would always change his mind. Those who admitted to knowing he was troubled also said that they had been sworn to secrecy at the time; they felt the need to respect Harley's wishes. Perhaps, deep down, they really didn't think he would actually go through with committing suicide. The sad truth, however, is that if Harley's parents had known what had been going through their son's mind—if only somebody had spoken up sooner—they may have been able to do something to help their son.

The guilt, pain, and all the unanswered questions became a major part of Janine and Ron's lives, even with such a large family surrounding them with as much love and support as they could give. Eventually, the couple decided it would be best to start seeing a counselor. Unfortunately, the counselor had never been touched by suicide before, and had no personal knowledge or understanding about what the family was going through. For that reason alone, Janine and Ron left their first appointment feeling even more depressed than before they had arrived. Suicide grief is so different from other kinds of grief. It can't be overcome by simply quoting from a textbook.

As Janine and I continued speaking of the past and what had happened, I asked my friend if she remembered an extra special time that she had spent with her son—a time before everything had gone so terribly wrong. She smiled and replied that it would have to be the time when she and her husband had planned a vacation. Harley was fourteen and Renee no longer lived at home. Leaving Renee behind, the trio went off to visit the sights of Tasmania. Looking back, she recalled that it was a happy occasion for each of them, a period where they were able to spend quality time with each other. Janine and Ron's attention had been fully focused on their son. Then Janine looked at me and noted that memories such as that have helped her, especially when there are moments when her thoughts take her back to the fight she had had with her son days before he had taken his life.

Janine and Ron have never been very religious. However, they have become more spiritual ever since their son's untimely death. There have been moments where they firmly believe Harley is letting them know he is with them. In particular, Janine spoke of a rose bush she had that she planted in early 2000, the same year of the Sydney Olympics. The rose bush was actually called "Olympic Gold" because of this. According to Janine, the bush had never flowered—that is, until the week her son died. Soon after, a beautiful yellow rose grew from the bush. One might think, *Well, so what? It was just a coincidence.* Janine likes to think otherwise.

On the first anniversary of Harley's death, Janine and Ron found nineteen perfectly formed yellow roses, and one that had only started to bloom, but then stopped. Coincidentally, Harley would have had his twentieth birthday three weeks later. Janine believes that this was no coincidence. With that, she and her husband picked the lovely bunch of roses and ventured out to place them on their son's grave. Now they call the yellow rose bush "Harley's Rose."

Approximately eighteen months after Harley took his life, Janine and Ron were still grieving the loss of their son. They decided to look further into what support was available for anyone on the Sunshine Coast who had lost a loved one to suicide. During their search, they discovered that very little help was out there. They also found that the stigma around suicide was still a *very* real issue. It was because of the terrible tragedy of losing their son in the way they did, and the lack of help and support around the area, that the courageous couple decided to try and seek out others to start a support group of their own. They figured that the support group could be available for anyone who needed it rather than have others go through the agony of trying to heal alone as they had.

Janine and Ron were fortunate to be able to make contact with a small group of people who were interested in starting a support group. Today, those folks make up our Standby team. It really didn't take a lot to set up our group; it just took the right people who were caring enough to make a difference.

I had been invited to attend that very first meeting. After the first few group meetings, Janine and Ron offered to start having the sessions at their home. Later, the group began calling itself Living Beyond Suicide. Taking the first step and attending those meetings was incredibly difficult at first. Walking into a place where you just don't want to be can be challenging, to say the least. Opening up to a group of strangers is even more of an

20

obstacle. However, Janine was the icebreaker for me. She had phoned me two days prior to the meeting, and we had talked and cried during our long conversation, exchanging stories and recalling memories of our lost loved ones.

At the time, I had lost both my sons to suicide and was still trying to come to terms with what had happened. I must admit that I had to be coerced by my doctor to make that initial contact, and that was only by allowing her to give my telephone number to Janine. But after my conversation with Janine, I was so grateful to have gathered enough courage to start attending the support group sessions. Meeting Janine and Ron—as well as Myrna, a wonderful, caring woman who volunteered to become our counselor and meeting facilitator—and the rest of the trauma team made me realize that there are people in the world who really *do* care enough to do something to help those in need. Their unwavering support helped me get to where I am today. Of course, I still grieve for the loss of my children and always will. But I made a choice to accept help from those who reached out, and doing so has made a huge difference in my life.

No one will ever know what really happened on that tragic day when Harley decided to take his life. To this day, what breaks Janine's heart the most is that she and Harley were fighting during the last time she ever saw her son alive. The harsh words the two of them exchanged are part of a memory that will forever be etched in her mind. The sad realization of never being able to change what was said out of angry frustration will always be with her. But if Janine holds on to the happier times, and continues reaching out to others in similar situations and surrounding herself with supportive people, she, too, will someday find the silver lining behind the dark clouds.

2. Dianna

Barbara's nightmare began on Thursday, October 17, 2002. However, she wouldn't realize that for several more days, believing she knew where her daughter, Dianna, was and what she was doing at the time. Dianna had been a student, and a major part of the thesis she had been working on involved her going out into the bush to study the elusive Eastern Ground Parrot. It wasn't unusual for her to be gone for extended days at a time.

Barbara began to recall Dianna's early childhood years. She and her husband adored Dianna, and so did her older sister, Paula. Dianna had been "the perfect baby," according to Barbara, and as the years passed, she continued to grow into a happy child who was very bright and artistic. Whenever Barbara and her husband hosted parties, Dianna would entertain all of the guests, making them laugh so much that sometimes they'd cry. She was quite the little entertainer, and everybody loved her.

Dianna was far from being an average child. At an early age, she proved to be extremely talented. She loved to dance, learning ballet at a very early age, and she also learned to play the piano. When she wasn't performing in one way or another, Dianna also enjoyed painting. Over the years, Dianna painted many beautiful pictures. In fact, her artwork eventually became her legacy, which offered some comfort to her family after Dianna decided to take her life.

At school, Dianna was an excellent student who excelled in every subject. After graduating high school, she went on to further her studies at the University of Queensland, St. Lucia, and eventually obtained a Bachelor of Science degree in animal research. Even though Dianna got along with all of her peers and had many friends, there were only two or three people who she was especially close with. Looking back, Barbara doesn't believe Dianna suffered from depression as a young girl; there was every indication that her daughter absolutely loved life.

However, Dianna had never been one to share her feelings about her health. Now Barbara believes her daughter's depression could have started while she was in college. Dianna was a conservationist—always interested in saving the environment—but sometimes she had to participate in the killing of animals as part of her studies. She'd be required to cut them open and dissect their brains. This used to upset Dianna terribly, and Barbara wonders if the impact had been too traumatic for her to overcome.

When Barbara and her husband got divorced, Dianna was twenty years old. She mostly stayed quiet, never letting her true feelings about their separation show. For most children, experiencing their parents' divorce is a devastating event for them; it is the end of the family as they know it. Even though Dianna was older and living away from home at the time, Barbara can't help but wonder just how much the break-up really *had* affected her daughter.

Dianna had been a beautiful young woman who was very petite with a fair complexion. She had large brown eyes that were incredibly expressive and full of passion, even if she did try to hide her real feelings from others. Dark, rich auburn hair surrounded her face, and whenever she grew her hair out long, it would cascade down her back in thick, gorgeous curls.

Dianna tried hard to portray herself as a happy, outgoing individual. She didn't want to come across as the unhappy young woman she truly was—someone suffering in so much pain and confusion. When Dianna finally earned her bachelor's degree, she felt completely drained from work. Additionally, her personal life was in turmoil, following a difficult break-up in a relationship that had gone wrong. It was understandable that Dianna was depressed, and her family understood this. However, her family also believed that it was a fairly normal stage for anyone to go through after ending a relationship. They assumed Dianna would get through the rough patch in her life and move on.

For Dianna, though, it was not so easy to move forward. She found herself at a crossroads, knowing that her journey was veering off the path she had originally planned to take. Her life was not what she had envisioned for herself. Feeling the need to get away from everything she had been involved in, Dianna decided to pack up some of her belongings and travel overseas. She explored parts of Europe, and then ultimately found a job in England for a short period of time. Later, she headed to Ireland where she became a nanny. When her services were no longer needed, she returned to England to care for an older woman before planning her return back home to Australia. Once in Australia again, she decided she would stay with her father in Brisbane for a while.

Dianna ended up spending a year overseas. During that time, her depression became so bad that she sought help from a doctor. Yet, she never let her family know she had gone to get treatment—or how badly she was hurting. Even after Dianna returned to Australia, she did not let her family know that she had been ill. Barbara and her family now believe that Dianna never followed up with another visit to her doctor. Instead, she had opted to self-medicate herself, trying to mask the pain. Unfortunately, like so many others who suffer from depression, she became an expert in hiding her illness—especially from those who loved her the most and probably could have helped.

In the last months of Dianna's life, she was doing something she really loved to do, which was studying life and helping to preserve it. She was teaching and doing research for a PhD at a local university, and she was also working on a thesis about a rare ground parrot called the Eastern Ground Parrot, a small green and speckled bird about the size of a cockatiel. It is an endangered bird that roosts, eats, and nests on the ground, making it rather vulnerable. The small parrot can only fly short distances—usually only three to six above the ground. It is mostly solitary and lives in dense sedgeland or heathland areas. There are three areas on the Sunshine Coast where they still remain, one of them being the Noosa National Park. Because of Dianna's studies, there were many times where she would have to go out into the dense bushland for days at a time. She knew that the little bird is so rarely seen, and their most active time is over a short period of approximately fifteen to twenty minutes.

While Dianna loved her work, her personal life was another story. Unfortunately, Dianna's ex-boyfriend worked at the same laboratory she worked at. The stress of seeing each other on a daily basis combined with Dianna's studies taking up so much of her time and energy made her start to feel depressed and out of control again. Life started to take its toll on her once more—both mentally and physically. Dianna decided to take another trip to get away from everything. With that, she made plans to go overseas once more. This time, however, she chose to visit Thailand. She would travel on her own as she had done before and then meet up with other travelers along the way.

In Thailand, Dianna's depression came back in full force, and she managed it the best she could without any of her fellow travelers catch on. But when she returned to Australia, she decided she needed to tell her mother how she was feeling. Barbara was relieved that her daughter confided in her and supported her in getting the help she needed.

As things returned to normal, Dianna seemed to be doing much better. When she went back to work, she took her supervisor's advice and transferred to another building away from her ex-boyfriend. This was not without difficulties, however. Barbara was aware of her daughter's transfer to another building. She also knew about Dianna's anxiety that came along with the transition. Yet, after seeing Dianna happier than she had been for a long time, and after hearing her daughter's doctor say that her medication was finally kicking in, Barbara relaxed and let her guard down a little.

Thursday, October 17, 2002, started out as a typical day. Barbara was home alone, waiting for Dianna to visit so they could write and send an email to Dianna's sister, Paula, who was on vacation overseas in Peru with her partner. Barbara's second husband, whom she had been married to for five years, was away on a fishing trip. When Dianna arrived around four thirty that afternoon, the two women talked for a while before going over to the computer and sitting down to compose their email. Never very good at spelling, Dianna made a joke to her sister in the email about all of her typos.

While Dianna typed away at the computer, Barbara wasn't aware that there was anything amiss with her daughter. The only difference in that visit versus all of the other times was that Dianna turned and said, "I love you, Mom." This was not something that was usually expressed between the mother and daughter, and Barbara told her daughter that she loved her, too. She then reminded her daughter to be vigilant about heathland fires; it was a hot and windy day. She knew the birds that Dianna was researching lived in quite inaccessible areas of dense scrub, and she realized how isolated her daughter would be. With that, Barbara hugged her daughter and stood in the doorway, watching, waving, and smiling as Dianna drove away. Little did she know that would be the last time she would ever see her daughter alive.

The next two days passed as normal for Barbara. Her husband returned home earlier than expected on Saturday night because he said the fish weren't biting. On Sunday afternoon, shortly before leaving the house to go have coffee with some friends, Barbara told her husband that she was expecting Dianna to call. She asked her husband to ask their daughter if she wanted to go over for tea that evening. When Barbara returned, however, and Dianna hadn't called yet, she wasn't unduly concerned. She simply thought Dianna was still busy with the birds or out doing something with her friends.

On Monday morning, Barbara and her husband attended their local Probus meeting. After the meeting, they headed to the grocery store to stock up on food. They wanted to prepare for guests that were arriving the following day. When they finally got back home, they unpacked their groceries and carried on as usual.

At five thirty that same afternoon, there was a sudden knock at the door. Barbara went to answer it. She was startled to see two policemen standing there with somber expressions on their faces. After identifying themselves, they asked Barbara if they could come in and speak with her. Barbara had no immediate thoughts of disaster; after all, it had been a perfectly normal day for her and her husband. As the officers followed her inside, she could only wonder what they could want.

Even after the police broke the news of a car and a body being found on the heath—and that they had reason to believe it was Dianna—Barbara didn't react to the news. Instead, she went and got her husband, who had been showering at the time. Barbara didn't believe for a minute that the body could be her beautiful daughter. After all, the police said the body could have been there for up to a week. She had last seen Dianna on Friday, just three days ago; they had to be wrong. (It was only later that Barbara realized the last time she had seen her daughter was that Thursday.)

As the traumatic news began to finally set in, Barbara felt her mind start to reel, especially when the police officers asked if Dianna had any dental records available. *They must have it all wrong!* Barbara thought. *This can't be happening! It just couldn't be Dianna, could it?* There was so much confusion all at once. Nothing made sense.

But later, after the police had left, Dianna's dear friend, Vicki, who was also her part-time employer and landlady, called the house. She had been trying to reach her friend since that morning. Vicki said she was concerned that Dianna had not been seen or heard from since she had left on her trip. When the police had been at the house, they had not told Barbara anything else other than that they believed they had found Dianna. Vicki's call made everything seem slightly more validated. With that, Barbara was forced to accept the possibility that the body found was indeed Dianna. However, there was no way she could believe that it might be suicide. *Murder or a snakebite? Maybe,* she thought. *There's no way she would've committed suicide, though.*

However, when Vicki told Barbara about letters that were left behind by Dianna, had no choice but to believe that Dianna had definitely taken her own life. Barbara's reaction to the horrific news was to be totally practical. For anyone who has ever been through this same kind of tragedy, it is completely understandable how she reacted. There were things that needed to be taken care of. Even though the disbelief of finding out Dianna had committed suicide was so uppermost in Barbara's mind, she knew she had to go on.

After calling the Noosa police to arrange to provide a statement the following morning, Barbara knew she had to start notifying her family. First, she had to call Dianna's father, who lived in Brisbane. She knew the news would totally devastate him, and she took comfort in the fact that he had a very loving and caring second wife to help him through what they all had to endure. Once Barbara's ex-husband was aware of what had happened, he attempted to contact Paula. However, he was unable to get in touch with them. He sent Paula an email, asking for her to contact him as soon as she could. It wasn't until a few days later that he was finally able to break the horrible news to the couple.

The severity of what had happened finally hit Barbara in the early hours the following morning. Dianna had left them forever. That's when the grief really started to set in. Barbara remembers sitting out in her garden, crying the first round of many tears to come. She wanted it all to just be a horrific nightmare where she would awake at any moment to just another ordinary day.

Morning eventually came, though, and Barbara's mind was still reeling. She would never again have the chance to see Dianna laugh or cry. She would never be able to say, "I love you." All of these thoughts broke her heart into a million pieces. Parents never expect to outlive their children, right? When it got a little later in the day, Barbara contacted her brother and let him know what had happened to Dianna. As the two of them spoke, it was decided that since both of Dianna's grandmothers were in their eighties, and her paternal grandmother was much too ill to handle such news, it would be best not to say anything to them. Barbara's brother would later tell Dianna's maternal grandmother what had happened once he returned home. He wanted to be able to break the news gently to her in person.

Barbara's family was not able to see Dianna because of the advanced state of decay that occurred to her body after being left to the mercy of heat and insects for three-and-a-half days. This is why the police officers had asked about dental records for identification. There were no dental records to be found, however, which was no surprise to Barbara, even though she and her husband did try to find some. Dianna had taken fluoride tablets as a child and never needed dental work. Ultimately, the coroner was able to positively identify Dianna when matched fingerprints from a drinking glass. After that, any chance of hope that Barbara clung to that the police officers had been mistaken was gone. The body that had been found really was her beloved Dianna.

Barbara and her family, with the help of Dianna's friends, were eventually able to piece together what had happened following Dianna's departure that last day. She had been able to drive into the heathland area at any time, having been issued with a set of keys to the gate in order to do her research. After entering the park, Dianna drove her car to a remote area that wasn't visible from the main fire track. After that, it is believed that Dianna pushed her way approximately one hundred feet through dense bush scrub to a place where she had previously been able to locate the Eastern Ground Parrot. She had with her a backpack containing the suicide notes for her family, a Walkman, a postcard, and some treasures from her childhood.

Additionally, she carried syringes and pentobarbitone, a barbiturate used to euthanize animals. She had enough pentobarbitone to successfully end her own pain. The police noted that they had found a pole used to string up mist nests, which are needed when catching the endangered birds, standing upright in the bush next to Dianna's body. The pole actually helped in locating her that Monday.

Not long after she arrived and set up camp, Dianna made three phone calls from her mobile phone. One was to her father to tell him that she loved him. She gave no hint as to why she wanted to say it at that particular time. The other two calls were made to the veterinary surgery house where she lived. The first was to ask if the assistant on duty could take care of her birds Friday and Saturday. A short while later, she called again, leaving a message for Barbara. She wanted to let her know that she would be on the heath and that the rangers would be able to find her "as she would stick out like a sore thumb." Unfortunately, both calls had been made after the office had closed for the day, and the assistant was unable to call Barbara the following morning because she did not have her current telephone number.

After making the final phone calls, Dianna's family and friends can only try to guess what happened next. When Dianna had arrived at her destination, it had been a hot afternoon. However, when her body was found, she had been wearing her Driza-Bone coat. It is believed that Dianna was probably still alive for some time during the night, even though the last phone call had been made before six o'clock that evening. At some point, she injected four syringes of the powerful drug into her body. Then she took the time to replace the caps on three of them.

That Monday morning, the vet's assistant went to speak to the veterinarian to say that the birds had not been attended to. She had been the one to feed them and change the paper in their cages that Saturday. That's when Vicki also became concerned after learning that Dianna had not arrived at a client's home on the Saturday night to take care of two cats as previously arranged. After finally finding Barbara's new phone number, Vicki tried to call Dianna's parents and let them know of her concerns. Unfortunately, Barbara and her husband had already left for their Probus meeting.

Unable to contact Dianna's parents, Vicki decided to contact a man named Rob, who was also a friend of Dianna's. At times, he had traveled into the heath with her. As it turned out, Rob told Vicki that he had been trying to phone Dianna over the weekend. However, he had not been able to reach her. That news made both of them even more alarmed, and Rob decided that he would go to an area where he knew Dianna had gone before. That location also happened to be the same place Dianna told her mother where she would be in her message.

When Rob found Dianna's locked car, he immediately called Vicki to let her know. Vicki then quickly contacted the police. Rob was the first person to see the mist net pole, and he was the first to see Dianna as well, even before the police arrived to secure the scene. The sight must've been traumatic for Rob, and Barbara believes he will probably never forgive Dianna for what she did to him that day.

Later, Barbara found a diary her daughter had left behind. The diary entries, mixed with what some of Dianna's close friends eventually divulged, allowed Barbara and her family to fill in a few gaps as to what was going through Dianna's mind before she decided to take her life. For starters, they gained a bigger picture of the depression Dianna had suffered for so many years. Then Barbara found a couple of other diaries that Dianna had left on her desk. She had recorded her battle with depression over the years, and wrote that she had unable to confide in anyone else about the anguish and pain she was going through. For some reason, however, she was able to write about her illness.

Barbara knew that her daughter had visited their family doctor about her depression approximately five years before her death. Dianna had told her mother that the medication she was prescribed made her feel "normal" for the first time in years. Barbara doesn't know why Dianna didn't continue with her medication, or why she didn't tell her doctor or the counselors she had seen just how severe her depression had been in the past. Because of this, they had all believed it was a one-off event; no one realized just how much pain Dianna was in.

In one of her diaries, Dianna wrote that she was "ashamed to let anyone know" what was inside her head. Barbara's anguish in reading her daughter's words was unbearable. It only made her ask herself over and over again the same question: *Why?* The internal questions were endless. *Why couldn't Dianna confide in someone? If not in me, then why not in a doctor or in one of her good friends? If she had, could it have made a difference?*

Barbara says she has no idea how she would have coped without the loving support of her husband, her brother and his wife, and her close friends after her youngest daughter's death, especially with her only other daughter overseas. Dianna's death was one of disbelief, despair, and unimaginable heartbreak. Even years after Dianna took her life, there isn't a day that goes by where Barbara doesn't think of her daughter. While she says coping with the pain *does* get easier with time, she's fully aware that it will never go away completely. She just desperately wishes things could've turned out differently.

Kaylene Donohue

I met Barbara through our *Living Beyond Suicide* group. I know that attending our support group has helped her tremendously. In a time of crisis like dealing with a suicide, it helps to know that you are not alone; other people truly *do* understand what you're going through. Barbara is a survivor, and she feels so strongly about what happened to her family that she has written a personal plea, which makes up the next chapter. She hopes that if anyone ever feels so low that he or she starts thinking about ending his or her own life, that person will read her plea and think about the devastation his or her actions would cause. Suicide really does have a continuing ripple effect.

3. Barbara's Plea

Perhaps, you've thought about committing suicide. Maybe you've seriously considered it. Or maybe you have actually decided to go ahead with it. You feel this is the only option you have. After all, ending your life will end the pain, the turmoil, and the complete chaos that your life has somehow become. Your pain is extreme, and it consumes your right now. It could be caused by any number of things—relationship failure, money problems, loneliness, or illness. You feel like you're looking at a black future. There's no light in sight. You don't believe that things can ever be good again. You have your reasons to want to end it all and leave all this behind. You want to go forward to peace, nothingness, or possibly, depending on your beliefs, another life—a chance to start over somewhere else.

But I beg of you, *please wait*. Please think! Please realize the magnitude of the pain, grief, suffering, and confusion that you would leave behind. Don't delude yourself. Your action will destroy the lives of those closest to you for years to come, and maybe forever. Your pain feels suffocating and unbearable now; theirs will be just as bad. Your depression will pass on to them. Add to that the guilt and the terrible loss they have to bear. There will be serious consequences for everyone who is close to you. *Their lives will never be the same again.*

They will be the ones who have to live with the shock and grief of your death, as well as the terrible guilt that they didn't see what was going to happen. They won't be able to get over the fact that they weren't able to help you. Your children, and even your siblings, will be more likely to take their own lives as a consequence. Please reconsider what you think you want to do. Know that you have options. Know that you will *always* have options.

There *is* hope for you. You can get help for your pain! Let your family, or professionals, or even your friends help you make things better. Persevere with your medication, if needed, and counseling. There is absolutely no stigma in needing help. You really can live through this terrible time and move on with those who would have moved on without you. Don't hand your pain and grief on to them. Don't ruin so many more lives. Above all, never underestimate the horrific effect that this irreversible action will have on all who are a part of your meaningful life. Nothing lasts as long as death.

They won't eventually "get over it" or ever forget. Instead, your loved ones will grieve for the rest of their days. Their health and wellbeing will be affected. The lives that are left behind will never be the same. I know this from my own personal, devastating experience. Please think about what you are considering. Please believe that your life is *valued* and *needed* no matter what you may be going through right now—it is!

Please don't end your life. It's forever . . . for everyone.

4. Ken

Pauline and Ken met when they both were working on Thursday Island. Pauline was a nurse; Ken was a schoolteacher. Being so far from home—and living on an island without a lot of inhabitants—it was inevitable that they would eventually meet and form a friendship. The couple's relationship blossomed quickly, though, and soon they realized that they wanted to spend the rest of their lives together.

After they married, Pauline and Ken started their new life in Bowen, a country town in Queensland. Living in a small country town usually means that everybody knows everybody. Bowen was a close community, and Pauline and Ken had many friends. They spent many happy years there, raising their three children. As Pauline reflected on those early days, talking about the man she loved so much, her eyes lit up. She added that Ken was a great man with a brilliant mind, who was always making her laugh. Their lives had been so perfect and complete. While every couple has an argument every now and then, that is not what Pauline remembers about her late husband. To her, Ken was constantly filling their home with laughter. He had been a joker and simply loved having fun.

As a father, Ken could not have done a better job. He was an excellent teacher, and he tried to teach his kids all he could. He truly enjoyed spending time with his children and doing things together as a family, including camping, fishing, and crabbing. It seemed he had boundless energy, never tiring of his responsibility as a parent or as a husband. Wherever Ken went, he proudly took his family with him. In fact, townspeople used to comment just how much Ken's family was together. They were always seen out doing some sort of activity.

How good would it be if life could go on that way forever? Unfortunately, that's not usually how the world works. For Pauline, Ken, and their children, the fairytale life they had been living would eventually crumble apart much too soon. Remembering what life used to be like is always hard. It's hard because you can never go back and try to fix what has already been broken, especially after a life is lost. It doesn't help knowing that, at the time, you believed you had done everything in your power that you could possibly do. Furthermore, it doesn't matter how much you try to help somebody. That person's journey is his or her own to take. If that person is not willing to accept or get help, you are powerless.

So when did Ken's life change? What made it change? Pauline had said he had been the perfect husband and father; he was larger than life. He had brought so much happiness to those whose lives he touched. He adored his life his family. What made him decide to take his life and lose all of that?

According to Pauline, her husband didn't change overnight. It was a slow process, which all started when Ken became ill. After Ken got sick, he needed to go on fairly strong painkillers. When they weren't enough to help ease his pain, he started to drink more than just socially with his friends. As the months passed, and Ken's pain worsened, so did his drinking. Soon after, circumstances forced him to leave his teaching job. Ken had loved being a teacher; he had been a teacher for most of his working life. Naturally, it was a huge blow to him when he had to give up the career he had enjoyed for so long.

Later, Ken got a new job working on a farm. It was, however, difficult for him to deal with the fact that his wife was suddenly the primary money-maker in their household. Ken started to become a worrier and critical of all those around him, especially his family. Pauline was painfully aware that her husband was in trouble and tried, with the help of family members, to get him some professional help. But Ken was stubborn, refusing to listen to anyone. Pauline and her family then tried to get him to move away from Bowen so they could make a new life somewhere else. Still, Ken would not budge.

Ken's health started to deteriorate more rapidly. At the same time, his drinking habit worsened. There came a point in his life where he felt he was unable to cope anymore. With that, he attempted to take his life by taking a bottle of pills. However, he was found in time and taken to the hospital. Unfortunately, there were no counselors or any kind of professional help available for Ken where he and his family lived. Furthermore, Ken was in complete denial that he had a problem. Following his release from the hospital, his life quickly spiraled downhill.

Feeling desperate and unable to watch Ken's self-destruction any longer, especially now that his actions were affecting their children, Pauline made a decision with her family's best interest in mind. She thought that the best thing to do would be separate from her husband and pack up and move to the Sunshine Coast of Queensland with her children in tow.

After their move, the family still kept in touch with Ken by regularly talking on the phone. The kids went to visit him during holidays, too.

Pauline continued to keep in touch with their friends, always wanting to know how Ken was doing. Their friends reported back that he seemed to be improving. In hindsight, Pauline now realizes that this is only what Ken wanted everyone to believe. In reality, he had been making his own plans.

With no family living near the Sunshine Coast, Pauline and her children were pretty much on their own. However, Christmas was always a busy time of year. With only a few weeks until Christmas, Pauline really wanted to try and make the holiday as happy as she could for her kids. It would be the first holiday they spent together without Ken there. In the short time since their move to the Sunshine Coast, Pauline and the kids had still been hopeful that Ken would miss his family enough to take control of his life and make the move as well. They had been such a strong family unit up until Ken started going downhill.

It was the thirteenth of December—days before Ken's fifty-first birthday—when Pauline received the worst news of her life. Ken had taken a gun to his head and ended his life. Pauline and her son, William, had been at home alone on that horrific day. When the phone rang the first time, it was one of William's friends back in Bowen; he had learned about Ken and wanted to check on William. However, after realizing that William hadn't heard the news yet, he said nothing about it and soon hung up. Again, since Bowen was such a small town, it was not long before the phone rang again. This time it was one of Pauline's friends who broke the devastating news of Ken's suicide.

As soon as she heard the words, Pauline's pain became so unbearable that she could hardly breathe. At the same time, she knew she had to contact her family and let them know what had happened. She had no idea if Ken's parents had been told yet. For the first time in her life, she felt so isolated from those who loved her, and she had no idea where to turn.

Pauline immediately called the one sister she knew would not be home alone. Her sister's husband answered the phone, and Pauline remembers trying to tell him what had happened. However, she was hardly able to get the words out of her mouth. When her brother-in-law finally understood what Pauline was trying to convey to him, he was in complete shock. Pauline's sister, who was standing beside him at that point, suddenly realized something terrible had happened and started trying to make sense of the phone call.

With the phone being the only way they could communicate with Pauline being so far away, it took a while before they all knew what had taken place. This is the kind of thing that should never happen—a family separated by distance, in so much pain and confusion, trying to communicate over the phone. It is never easy to break bad news to someone, but it helps if you have somebody beside you or to at least to make that difficult call for you.

The police were no help; they did not have the information needed to contact the Standby trauma team, which had—once again—been very much needed at that time. The closest friends Pauline had nearby were a couple who had taught school at Bowen. They had known Ken, Pauline, and their family, and Pauline was able to contact them for help. With only William at home, she had to then get her two daughters, Sammy and Cassie, to return home. Sammy was away for the weekend, and Cassie had been at a friend's house. Both girls knew as soon as they were contacted and told they needed to come home immediately that something terrible had happened. However, neither of them had been prepared to hear that their father had taken his life.

Pauline's sister left Melbourne as soon as she could book a flight. Still, it took quite a bit of time before she was able to get to the Sunshine Coast and be there for Pauline and her kids. As for Pauline, even with going through shock and confusion, she knew she had to make plans to drive the long trip back to Bowen. She needed to bury her husband—the father of her children and man she had thought she would spend the rest of her life with. She also knew she had to tie up loose ends with their home. There would be a lot of big decisions to make.

Pauline feels very fortunate in having always had such a close relationship with Ken's family. Knowing about Ken's problems, they had always been very supportive of her and how she was trying to handle everything. With the news of Ken's death, she knew they would try and help her and her children through the hardest time of their lives. In fact, Pauline and her children stayed with Ken's family for a night on that long journey back to Bowen.

After Pauline's sister tried to find some professional help for her family, she eventually found information about Standby. She quickly contacted that team and was connected with some wonderfully caring counselors. The counselors then were able to go and spend a long time with the family, trying to help them through their terrible nightmare. Trauma teams are trained to specialize in helping after a suicide happens. They have the ability to give the right kind of information and support. Pauline says she had called Lifeline and that Sammy had gone to see a counselor after Ken's death; however, those resources weren't for them in the end. They were not suicide-specific so they could not give Pauline and her daughter what they needed most.

At the time of Ken's death, Pauline had been working at a nursing home in Caloundra. Upon hearing the devastating news, she was able to take two weeks off from work to attend the funeral and take care of matters with the house. Unfortunately, she was unable to be given any additional time off after that; the nursing home was short-staffed. Pauline returned to work after her two-week break, but she quickly found she was unable to cope with what had happened. She had difficulty just trying to function normally from day to day.

Eventually, Pauline's extended family returned to their homes and their lives. After that, Pauline and her children were left to manage the best way they could. Even after some time passed, leaving the house was still terribly hard. Pauline found that every time she walked out the door, tears would start streaming down her face. Pauline knew that she needed to try and get back into a normal routine, if not for herself, then at least for her kids. After arriving at her workplace, she would dry her eyes and force herself to get through another day. At the end of her shift, she would get into her car, break down all over again, and drive to her house. Once at home, she would quickly dry her tears and put on a brave face before going inside to see her children.

The counselors who had gone to visit Pauline and her family had also given them the address and telephone number of our support group. One day, taking all the courage she could muster, Pauline drove over to Janine and Ron's home to sit in on a group meeting. Feeling scared and very vulnerable, she parked her car and walked to the door. She knew that she was exactly where she needed to be. During that first meeting, she remembers walking in and sitting beside me. She also remembers that there were plenty of tears. However, for the most, the meeting was a complete blur.

To this day, Pauline believes that she and her children are very fortunate to have been living on the Sunshine Coast when she was. She thinks that if she had still lived in Bowen when Ken committed suicide, she would have crawled into a hole and stayed there forever, digging herself in deeper without finding any way out. Furthermore, she doesn't know if her kids would've turned out to be the confident, happy young adults they are today. Pauline also thinks that the statistics saying that a suicide affects eight to ten people out of each family are definitely inaccurate; there were well over three hundred people at Ken's funeral. His death impacted all of them in some way. In Pauline's extended family alone, many people needed ongoing counseling to get through their grief.

As time went on, Pauline felt her son, William, was bottling up his emotions, and she knew that wasn't healthy. She had been concerned that he could be heading for trouble if he didn't talk to someone. The Standby team offered Pauline a contact for her son. Soon, William began attending meetings through Gaining Ground, a group run by a special team at Child-Informed Mediation Study (CIMS), which focuses specifically on trying to improve children's mental health. After attending this group, William began to start to turn his life around. He was even asked to be a speaker to try and help other young kids going through what he had experienced.

5. Sammy's Story

Samantha, or Sammy as her family and friends call her, had been having a great life before her father, Ken, suddenly committed suicide. She loved to party and even described herself as "a little on the wild side." Very little ever worried Sammy, and for the most part, she remembers growing up in a happy home with her younger siblings, Cassie and William, and loving parents. Like Sammy's mother, Pauline, had said, Sammy thought that Ken had been an exceptional father, always taking his children to fun places. She remembers how he often made his family laugh.

Sammy admits that she doesn't really remember when her dad started to change. Being just a child, she was unaware of the problems that had started to occur when her father first became ill. As Ken liked to drink, it wasn't unusual for Sammy to see him with a beverage in his hand. Even though she eventually realized that her dad was drinking more than he typically did, she hadn't thought of it as being or becoming a major problem. It was only months later, after Ken's health had further deteriorated, that she realized something was going on.

Sammy remembers the looks her family would get from the towns-people of Bowen whenever they were out and about together. People seemed to admire their family. However, the same people who once used to comment on how close their family had been were suddenly looking at them in a very different manner. It was as if they almost pitied the family. To Sammy, it was an uncomfortable feeling.

When things got really bad, Sammy moved to the Sunshine Coast with her mother and two siblings. Their mother was determined to start a new life for them, even if it had to be without their father. Still, he was still very much a big part of their lives. Ken would often call his children to see how they were doing. Additionally, they would make plans to see him during holidays and school breaks. Whenever Sammy and her siblings met up with their father, they would try to catch up on some of the things they used to enjoy doing. Even though there were miles that separated them, they all tried to maintain a close relationship. Ken was still their father, after all.

When Pauline and Ken decided to take a break from each other, the whole family hoped it would not be a permanent decision. In fact, Pauline and the kids had tried convincing Ken to join them on the Sunshine Coast for many months. While there was still the possibility that this could ultimately happen, Sammy and her siblings always believed their dad would be there for them no matter what, just like he always had been.

For Sammy, having a dad as a schoolteacher certainly had its good points. Ken had pushed his kids hard, teaching them all he could to try and give them a good education. He always encouraged them to do the very best they could. This was all a great help when the kids had to change schools; they were able to do so without too much difficulty. The hardest thing had been leaving all their friends in Bowen behind.

It was easy for Sammy to start making new friends, though. She was young, pretty, and outgoing. It didn't take long for her to find a group of girls and start hanging out with them. Unfortunately, her life was about to change in a way that would take her on a journey that she would never have believed possible.

Sammy and her friends had been looking forward to spending the weekend away on Bribie Island, not far from the Sunshine Coast where they lived. As Sammy set off to join her friends, she was carefree and happy. They had all planned to have a great time celebrating an eighteenth birthday party of one of their friends, and the partying was well underway. However, the moment Sammy's mother called her cell phone and told her she needed to come straight home, Sammy had a gut feeling that something was terribly wrong.

The trip home felt like it took forever. All kinds of things raced through Sammy's mind. The thought that something had happened to her dad did cross her mind, but she quickly pushed it aside, thinking she was just tormenting herself and being paranoid. But the moment she got home and her mother told that her father had taken his life, Samantha's own life fell apart. The pain was excruciating. She just could not comprehend that she would never see her dad again. *How will I go through life without my dad?* she wondered. She had always assumed her dad would be there when she needed him, and now he was gone. How was she supposed to cope? The whole ordeal was heart-wrenching and too unbearable to think about.

In the weeks following Ken's death, life was pretty much a blur for Sammy. She was filled with so much pain that she didn't know how to handle. She went through the motions of what needed to be done but was in a daze. Traveling to Bowen for her father's funeral was the hardest thing Sammy ever had to do. However, she knew it needed to be done. Later, when it came time to scatter her father's ashes, Sammy was unable to go back to Bowen to participate. She couldn't bring herself to go back to the town that previously had so many good memories—until now.

Sammy's life literally changed forever after her father took his life. Not knowing how to cope with her feelings, she went to see a counselor. Unfortunately, the counselor she went to did not have any training in dealing specifically with suicide, which meant that Sammy was unable to deal with her emotions in an effective way. Unless somebody is either trained or has lost some one to suicide, it is very hard for that person to be able to help. They simple don't have the knowledge or understanding about what the person who is dealing with the aftermath of suicide is *really* going through.

Sammy was deeply affected by her dad's death. It was difficult for her to get her words out without having tears suddenly start streaming down her face. When I spoke with her, she told me that if her dad couldn't do it—if he had found life to be too hard to live—then how could she and her siblings be expected to get through their own lives? Clearly, Ken's death left a major void, and Sammy desperately wanted him back. She *needed* him to be in her life. Who was going to walk her down the aisle when she got married one day? Nobody could replace him. Then there would be the time when she hopefully had children. Sammy had believed her dad would be there to be a grandfather and a role model, teaching her children the way he had taught his own.

Sammy realized that so much would be done differently now because her dad wouldn't be there anymore. In a way, Ken's death had ended Sammy's childhood. She was forced to grow up very fast and certainly not the way she had wanted. At the same time, however, Sammy now has a new respect for life. Because of her father's death, she has chosen to go down other paths rather than the one she was headed the day she received the terrible news.

Approximately five months after Ken died, I got to meet Sammy, Cassie, and William in person. That day tore at my heartstrings, reminding me of my two children and how they were profoundly affected by their older brother's suicide. It was heartbreaking to see the pain and confusion in their eyes, even months after their father had passed away. I also knew that their vulnerability could potentially send them down paths that were not good for them. I left that day, trying to get them out of my mind. That quickly proved to be unsuccessful.

After a long healing process, Pauline, Sammy, Cassie, and William were eventually able to move forward. One day, I called Sammy to see if she was interested in helping set up a young people's support group. Sammy, Cassie, and William actually became the core of that group, and to this day, they still participate whenever they are able to. The group gave them something positive to focus on in their lives. When trying to come up with the name for our young people's group, they ultimately decided on calling it "Head High." They thought the name seemed fitting for themselves and all the other kids in a similar position. Despite having to deal with such a tragedy, kids still have the ability to hold their heads up high. Those impacted by their loved ones' actions need to know that they have nothing to be ashamed of.

6. Cassie's Story

Cassie remembers a happy childhood, growing up with an older sister, a younger brother, and loving parents who were always there for her and her siblings. Cassie has lots of happy memories of her family at home and from when they went on different outings. Looking back, Cassie would describe her father as being a typical Aussie—always having his hat on his head, his dog beside him, and a cooler full of beer somewhere nearby. Even though Cassie's dad was a schoolteacher, who tended to be pretty tough on his own children in an attempt to try and teach them as much as possible, he was also a big softy. Cassie recalls times when her dad would let her and her siblings skip school just so that he could take them fishing, which he often loved to do.

Once Cassie's parents decided to split up, packing up and moving to the Sunshine Coast with her mother and siblings was hard. However, Cassie still maintained a close relationship with her dad. It was nowhere near the same as it had been when the family lived together, but she was still able to see her dad during holidays, and she spoke often with him on the phone. As Cassie told me her version of the story, her demeanor shifted. It was evident that the day Cassie lost her father to suicide will be forever etched in her memory. It was a day that changed her life forever, the beginning of a real-life nightmare.

Cassie had been out with a girlfriend when she received a call from her mother, letting her know that she was needed at home immediately. Her mom added that somebody would be coming to pick her up. Cassie remembers that her thoughts immediately turned to her dad without knowing why. Her mind began to race as she wondered what was going on.

As soon as she was brought to her house, she ran inside and walked up to her mother. Pauline took her by the shoulders and looked her straight in the eyes. "Your father is dead," she blurted. Cassie remembers tearing herself away from her mother's grip and running into her bedroom. She then fell onto the bed, grabbed one of her pillows, and pushed her face into it. After that, she started screaming. A little while later, her mother entered the bedroom and sat on the bed next to her. She took Cassie in her arms, and the two of them just hugged each other and cried for a long time. Both of them were desperately trying to gain what comfort they could from each other in such a painful time.

Cassie didn't ask any questions until later that night when she sat down with her mother and siblings. That's when their mother told them what had happened to their dad. It is such a shock when you first hear about someone you know and love taking his or her life. Your mind suddenly explodes with so much pain and confusion that the world around you, in a way, ceases to exist. Everything becomes fuzzy—just a hazy fog that envelops you. For Cassie and her family, it was no different. They were instantly thrown into a place they never dreamed they would be.

Cassie doesn't remember a lot about the weeks following her dad's death. However, she remembers her aunt and grandmother coming up from Victoria. She also remembers her aunt contacting the Standby team, and someone coming out to see the family. Everything else, though, remains hazy. It was a very painful and confusing time for Cassie; her mind probably shut out some of the bad memories.

Soon after, Cassie began going through the various stages of grief: denial, anger, bargaining, depression, and acceptance. She remembers being incredibly angry and mentally beating herself up because she never saw her father's suicide coming. She wondered if she had, then maybe she could have done something to prevent her father's death. Eventually, Cassie learned that everybody within her family had very different feelings at very different times as they, too, went through the grieving process. She realized that it was okay; people are all different and get through traumatic times in their own ways.

For some, "anger" is a natural way to react because we don't understand *why* some people choose to commit suicide in the first place. *Why didn't that person say something? Why didn't I see that something was wrong? Why didn't I do something to fix it?* Unfortunately, these questions only create more confusion in our minds. We all hurt when we suddenly face something life-changing like this, but we all don't necessarily show our feelings in the same way.

Cassie says there are times when something in her everyday life will trigger a certain memory she has of her father, like the simple smell of toast being made. Normally, these little things wouldn't make her think twice, but sometimes she suddenly gets an overwhelming flood of emotions as she's brought back to happier times when her father was alive. On one particular day, the smell of toast reminded her of a relaxing morning at home when her family all lived together. Her dad had often made toast when she woke up in the morning. Cassie doesn't know what triggered that memory on that day, or why she can be having a good day and then suddenly her mind fills up with memories of her dad—and sometimes of what happened.

Another experience like that was in the first week that Cassie returned to school after her father's death. She walked into the classroom as usual, but she also wasn't smiling. Her teacher, oblivious to what Cassie had gone through, glanced over at her and said, "Cassie, smile, would you? It's not like anyone has died or anything!" Cassie was shocked by what her teacher said. With that, she quietly sat in her seat and stared at him, thinking, *You have no idea.*

I can guarantee that there will be times when people say things like Cassie's teacher either because they simply don't know or because they are thoughtless. These things will always happen, and chances are, you will feel upset and angry at the person who says the wrong thing at the wrong time. It had been difficult for Cassie to return to school and keep quiet about what had happened. Nobody knew about her circumstances. If they had, those unintentionally cruel words would never have been spoken by Cassie's teacher.

Luckily, with the help of the trauma team and the Head High support group, Cassie was later able to come to understand that it had been her father's decision to take his life. She had absolutely no control over what had happened. Even so, Cassie still feels regretful for not spending more time with her dad, especially the last time she had visited him. Instead of going fishing with her dad and her brother, she had chosen to go shopping with her best friend. While she knows she had no way of knowing that would be the last opportunity to spend quality time with her dad, she still also realizes she can never change that.

Cassie loved her dad with all her heart and will never blame him for what he went through. She says that she also will never blame him for choosing to leave their family. There will be many times throughout Cassie's life where she will miss her dad, especially those times where there will be nobody else who can take his place. The first big hurdle was her high school graduation, one of the most important moments in Cassie's life. She also had to sit out during the father-daughter dance. Even though Cassie's mother sat beside her, it wasn't the same. They both watched the dance without saying anything, both painfully aware why Ken was not there.

Cassie says she doesn't look forward to graduating from college and having to go through the same thing all over again. However, she adds that if it wasn't for her dad and all he had taught her, she would not be so strong-willed and determined to finish her studies. Regardless of what happened, she is forever grateful for the brief role her father played in her life. Another milestone that Cassie isn't looking forward to is getting married. The thought of Ken not being there to walk Cassie down the aisle is painful; Cassie doesn't even want to think about it. Sometimes she wonders if she won't marry at all. Other times she thinks that if she does, she will just go overseas.

Despite such a major setback, Cassie was able to push through and finish her schooling. At the same time, she began playing an active role in the Head High organization with her two siblings. Cassie's involvement in Head High has been a great healing power, both for herself as well as for others. It has encouraged her to be positive, and it has also helped her to be able to talk about her father and what had happened. She was able to understand as much about what happened as she could, which then enabled her to start the necessary healing process. Additionally, Head High also helped Cassie a long way in achieving some of the goals that she wanted to achieve. She found a job of her liking, in a resort, giving her the opportunity to work overseas. Her job included extensive travel, during which she met her life partner, with whom she is now leading a happy married life, with the addition of a little baby boy to the family.

7. Adam

Tania read a story in the local newspaper about Head High—our young people's support group for kids who have lost loved ones to suicide—which prompted her to pick up the phone and give me a call. She was desperate for help. At the time, our trauma team still was fighting for funding; unfortunately, they were unable to do much at all in terms of offering assistance.

As we talked, Tania explained that her step-son, Adam, had taken his life some weeks before, leaving his wife and four young children alone. She had made many phone calls to various organizations, trying to find somewhere to go for support. However, only after reading the newspaper article about Head High did she finally find anything to do with support groups that specifically focused on people dealing with suicide.

When Tania finished telling her story, I asked if she would like me to go see her and her family. She immediately said yes, sounding relieved. With that, she gave me her address and I hopped in my car. I knew only too well the pain and confusion the family was still going through. It didn't matter that weeks had passed since Adam had taken his life. It was still so very raw for them—and would be for a long time.

I knew Adam's family would be going through many different stages of grief. They'd be experiencing intense feelings that nobody would really understand unless they, too, had gone through coping after a suicide. They would have an infinite amount of unanswered questions: *Why? Why? Why?* Sadly, they would never receive the answers they were looking for. I also knew they would still be immersed in a fog where denial can be all too easy. Admittedly, it was hard not to take myself back to the time when my only daughter had also taken her life just a few short months earlier.

I remember getting out of the car and walking up to the door. After ringing the doorbell and waiting for a few seconds, a woman opened the door at smiled at me. It was Tania. We briefly said hello and introduced ourselves, and then I walked right up to her and gave her a big hug. After that, I was invited into her home. One of the first things I noticed was a Christmas tree, complete with decorations and presents all around it. However, the atmosphere was anything but festive.

As I walked a little further into the room, I saw a group of people, including a young boy who was asleep on a made-up bed on the floor. He was the youngest child. Mel, Adam's wife, was sitting on another made-up bed near him. Beside her was a young girl who appeared to be approximately five years old. As we all introduced ourselves, two young girls around the age of fifteen also came into the room. One of the girls identified herself as Jenny, Adam's oldest child. She was a slim young girl with dark hair. Even though it was almost noon, she was still in her pajamas. The other teenager was her friend.

After saying hello to Mel and giving her a hug, I turned toward Jenny and smiled. As I took her hand and gazed into those large blue eyes that were so full of unshed tears, I could see how much she was hurting. The sight of her with all her confusion made it difficult for me to hold back my own tears. Suddenly, I felt very protective of the young girl, like I wanted to wrap Jenny up in a warm blanket so nothing else could hurt her.

I later found out that Jenny was Adam's daughter through his first marriage. When Adam took his life, leaving her behind, Jenny felt as if her father had abandoned her. Naturally, she was devastated. It was almost too much for her to bear—the loss of the person she had loved most in this world.

I stayed with the family for some time just talking to them about the help that was available, trying to give them some kind of hope that life would get better. I must add again that it was during this time that our Standby trauma team was virtually non-existent due to lack of funding. Had things been different, I would have given Tania that telephone number to call so that specially qualified counselors would have been able to go out to their home and offer the family the help they so badly needed. Instead, I was able to give them information about our support groups. I let them know that if they wished to attend, they were very welcome to do so. I also made myself available to them if they needed me for whatever reason—even if it was to just stop in and say hello, letting them know they were not alone.

Over the next few months, I made sure to keep in touch with the family, calling every now and then to see how things were going. Jenny came to one of our Head High meetings, and Tania and Mel attended one of our *Living Beyond Suicide* support group meetings. Life around that time was incredibly busy, especially with some of the group members banding together, trying to get the members of Parliament to realize how important the Standby trauma team was. Funding had finally run out, and there were many families who were desperately in need of help and support. However, the team was only able to do what they could via the telephone. In many cases, families badly needed their actual presence.

It was some time before I was able to catch up with Tania again. When I finally did reach out to her, I learned that Mel had taken the children back to Victoria where they were originally from. Tania herself was not able to attend our group because of work commitments. It was a huge surprise, then, when she contacted me out of the blue one day to let me know Jenny was living with her again. She was hoping that Jenny would be able to attend our Head High meetings again.

Jenny came along to our next meeting, and she participated in doing some art with the group. Eventually, she relaxed and opened up a little. Of course, our puppy, Sophie, was there to help break the ice. In fact, Sophie ultimately became Head High's mascot. To this day, I truly believe that she knows just how important her role is in making the kids all feel welcome during our meetings.

It is just as important for children as it is for adults to understand that they are not alone when suicide hits close to home. There are also many other kids out there who have lost someone they love to suicide. Head High plays an important role in teaching kids many things, including that what happened was never their fault; that they have nothing to be ashamed of; and that they are definitely not alone. In many cases, I believe *how* these kids cope with their loss determines how they will continue their own journeys. Kids are very easily influenced, especially when they are vulnerable during stressful, traumatic times. That's why it is so important to offer them the proper resources and support as soon as possible.

Additionally, we should always try to be aware of how those closest to us are doing. Sometimes adults become so preoccupied in their own lives that they do not see what is going on in their children's lives. I am really stressing this point because I firmly believe that if the right support was around at the time my eldest son, Terry, decided to take his life, I am sure our lives would be much different today.

8. Anna

If you were to hear of an eighty-three-year-old woman taking her life, you would probably be inclined to think, *Well, I bet it was euthanasia.* However, in this case, you would be wrong. As Marianne and I sat together in comfy chairs, quietly chatting, I looked out the window at the beautiful view she wakes up to every day. When I returned my gaze to Marianne, I could almost see her sadness in not being able to persuade her mother, Anna, to come and live with her and her husband, to share in the wonderful peace and serenity. Marianne believes that if her mother had just given herself a chance to come and stay, the last years of her life may have turned out much differently.

Before Marianne began to talk about her mother, she started off by telling me how some of her family, and even her extended family, may perceive Anna's life to have been very different from how she saw her mother's life. However, this is the way Marianne remembers some of what happened from her very own memories, and also from the gaps her mother was able to fill in for her over the years. This is *her* story.

Anna was born in Breslau, Germany, in 1923. Marianne doesn't know much about this part of Anna's life, yet she believes that her mother had a great childhood. Her parents had been quite wealthy; therefore, life would have been good to her. Anna's father had been a pilot in World War I, flying in the same squadron as the very famous Red Baron.

Anna was only sixteen when World War II began. Adolescents of both sexes had been encouraged—and almost ordered—to join the Hitler Youth. For young girls, it was called the Bund Deutscher Mädel, or the BDM. which was also known as the League of German Girls. It would have been an exciting time for Anna because of the comradeship with lots of other young people and learning to do many amazing things. In fact, she gained the skills to one day sew a beautiful satin and lace bridal gown for her daughter and both of her daughter's bridesmaids' dresses. She also learned how to repair vacuum cleaners and other small home appliances if ever they suddenly had problems. Most importantly, however, she was taught how to become independent, and that was something that would benefit Anna throughout the rest of her life.

We all now know of the terrors and atrocities that befell the Jews during World War II. Many Germans were ordered to do things that went against everything they believed in. They survived the war, only to be traumatized from their experiences and not at all proud to be a member of the German race. Anna was one of those people. At a very young age, she was among many young people who joined to serve under the leadership of Adolf Hitler, not realizing at the time what a monster the Germans' leader was.

Anna never liked discussing the war or what happened, but in one rare conversation with her daughter, she spoke of a time when she had to supervise women prisoners who worked in the salt mines. Sadly, she mentioned how the women had been so thin and undernourished; yet Anna was never allowed to show any kindness toward them. There was one occasion, though, when Anna had taken some food for her own consumption. She placed it in a small partitioned area of the mine. Before needing to go and relieve herself, she indicated to three female workers that they could have the food. She told them to share it quietly and not draw attention to themselves. When Anna returned, she realized that the women had fought over the food; they did the very thing she had asked them not to do! This brought retribution on herself for trying to share her food, and the three young women were taken away. Anna never saw them again.

Anna must have seen some horrific things during the war. Those traumatic memories were etched into to her memories for the rest of her life. They were memories that were so unbearable that she would never speak about the war or even watch movies that involved any kind of war scenes. The one good thing that did come out of those trying times, however, was Gerhard, the man Anna met and fell in love with.

At the end of the war, Anna and Gerhard got married. Anna was twenty-two years old. Gerhard had made it home from the war, but he was badly injured and lost his right leg during combat on the front line. Ironically, his brother had been fighting on the Russian front that same day. He was also badly wounded and lost his left leg. Unfortunately, Gerhard's brother ended up dying after gangrene set in. He never had the chance to return home.

Once Anna and Gerhard were married, they went back to live with Gerhard's family on their farm. For a while, the newlyweds were very happy working on the farm. Later, they became the proud parents of a beautiful baby daughter. As it can happen, though, when living and working with families, problems do occur. Until the war, Anna had never needed to work or even worry about money. It must have been hard for her—moving away from everybody and everything she knew and loved—to follow the man she had fallen in love with. She had become strong during the war, and it was this strength that must have given her the courage to follow the path that she wanted to take and leave her privileged life behind.

Gerhard began to find it difficult to work on the farm with his one leg, and Anna did not really get along with his family. For these reasons, the young couple began making plans to move elsewhere. Soon, they headed off to begin their new life together with their young daughter.

Anna and her husband were happy in their new life, and it was not long before they found out that they were expecting another baby. Everything was going as planned. But one day, Anna took a bad fall. That one incident tragically and suddenly changed everything for Anna and her little family. Anna was taken to the hospital due to complications with her pregnancy. It wasn't until then that doctors realized that she had been expecting twins. When it was time to give birth, one of the twins was stillborn. Although the other baby survived, she was very ill.

Gerhard used to visit Anna in the hospital every day, riding his bicycle in a style that suited his disability. However, when he didn't show up one afternoon, and he didn't come the next day, Anna became very worried. That just wasn't like her husband. With that, Anna discharged herself from the hospital to go she and see where Gerhard was. Deep down, she knew something must have happened.

When Anna arrived home, she found Gerhard in the house, and he was very sick. Apparently, he had fallen off his bicycle on his way to the hospital and injured the stump of his amputated leg. Gerhard had been able to return to their home, but he was unable to go and seek help. His injury only worsened over time. Without medical attention, the fluid caused from Gerhard's injury had become so dangerously high that it had built up and spread quickly throughout his body. By the time Anna found her husband, he was already drowning in his own fluid. Anna rushed over to him, and he died in her arms before she could get him up and to the hospital. It was a terrible trauma for Anna to go through—one that her daughter believes made a big impact on the rest of her life.

In just a matter of days, Anna had lost one baby as well as her beloved husband. Meanwhile, her newborn daughter, the surviving twin, was fighting for her life. The baby needed a complete blood transfusion to help her to survive, and her blood type was rare to find. Anna was at a loss, not knowing where to turn. So much had changed in such a short period of time.

Anna decided to go for a walk to clear her mind. She went to a nearby park and sat down on a bench. Soon after, she began to sob uncontrollably, thinking about her husband and the twin who didn't survive. She hoped with all her heart that the second twin would miraculously get better. While she was sitting on the bench, a young African-American soldier sat down beside her. He asked if she needed help. Anna then told him about her husband's recent death. She also told him about her surviving newborn daughter, who was fighting for her life in the hospital. She added that she needed a blood transfusion, but she had a rare blood type.

Just like that, Anna had one of her prayers answered. The young man told her that he had the same blood type as the baby. He didn't hesitate to offer to see if his blood could be used to save the baby. He was more than willing to help if he could, especially if that meant Anna's baby could be able to live a normal, healthy life.

Gerhard's body had been taken back to his family, and a funeral was held soon after. Anna had gone back to stay with Gerhard's family until she recovered enough to continue on with her two daughters. It must have taken incredible strength for Anna to undertake a trip with two small children in tow. They had to cross a border that was manned by many soldiers—and Anna didn't have the necessary pass to get through. Even though the war was over, there were still many checkpoints throughout Germany. The Berlin Wall was just being built.

Marianne remembers her mother telling her that when Anna left the farm for the last time, she had set out on foot, pushing a baby carriage with her baby inside with one hand while her other daughter walked beside her. Anna took with her all she could carry in her other hand. It took two-and-a-half days of walking through bushland to arrive at the checkpoint Anna needed to cross. Without a pass, this incredible lady somehow got the guards to believe she had been visiting family across the border and was returning home. However, she actually wanted to go in the opposite direction! Luckily, her plan worked, and the guards told her she had to go back. With that, Anna hurried down the road with her two small daughters to start the next part of their journey together.

Eventually, Anna found a small apartment, and things started looking up for her again. Anna was still young and beautiful; she still had so much life to live. She loved the social scene, and liked to party and have fun just like any normal young woman. It was during one of these outings where Anna met a man named France. He was not a very tall man, and he wasn't exactly handsome, but he caught Anna's attention with his bright red hair and his love for dancing. When France and Anna started dancing, he made her feel like she was the only one in the world. Soon, Anna found herself falling in love with France, and he eventually moved in with her and her two daughters.

The months that followed were happy for Anna. She believed she was incredibly lucky to get a second chance at love and happiness. To add to her happiness, Anna found out she was pregnant. Before she had a chance to tell France the joyous news, though, cruel fate stepped in once again. Anna had been enjoying a drink in a café. She was impatient for the day to end so she could go home and share the wonderful news with France. Before leaving the café, however, she overheard a conversation between some women. Apparently, France and a woman Anna knew well were having an affair. Anna was devastated to learn that France had been cheating on her. Feeling numb with pain, she made her way. When she finally got there, she immediately packed France's things and coldly told him to leave.

The sudden break-up was hard for Anna. She had two small daughters and was now expecting another baby—and she was alone again. Eventually, France learned of the pregnancy, but Anna chose to tell him the baby wasn't his. Lying must have been a really hard decision for her to make, and it was something she would have to live with forever. She figured it was for the best, though.

When Anna moved into the apartment building, she quickly became friendly with some of the other tenants and their families. One of her friends was a widower named Karl. He had four young children. Karl needed some-one to watch over his kids while he was at work, and so he and Anna made an arrangement where she would care for his family for a small fee. This arrangement worked well, and Anna and Karl eventually grew much closer, confiding in each other their hopes and dreams.

As Anna's pregnancy progressed, it became harder for her to walk the two stories up and down to take care of Karl's children. After coming home late one night and finding Anna asleep on the couch, Karl decided to just let her sleep. Soon after, Karl decided the right thing to do was to ask Anna to marry him. Anna said yes.

The couple did eventually marry after Anna had given birth to her third daughter, Marianne. Even though Karl was a lot older than Anna, and they weren't in love, they did like and respect each other. Most of all, their seven kids now had two parents. The family lived in the same apartment for quite a few years. When it was time for the eldest child, Karl's son, to leave the nest, he immigrated to Australia. After sending many letters home to his family about how good life was in Australia, Anna and Karl finally decided to make the move to Australia as well.

The family traveled over to Australia in one of the many ships that carried immigrants to the new country. Ultimately, Anna and Karl settled in Tasmania with their family. Karl found work as a butcher while Anna took care of the children like she had always done. Unfortunately, as the months went on, the couple's marriage started to fall apart. As mentioned, the couple hadn't married for love; it had been a marriage of convenience because of their circumstances. They deserved credit for trying to make it work, but two years after their move to Tasmania, Anna and Karl separated and later divorced. Once again, Anna found herself alone with her three daughters.

Anna was never afraid of having to fend for herself and her family. She was still in her thirties when she found a job as a nurse. She also took a job working in a bar to help make ends meet. She never gave up. The one thing Anna needed most in her life, though, was somebody to love and have that person love her just as much in return. Unfortunately, she was always attracted to the wrong kind of man.

Allan soon entered her life. Even though Anna knew he was married, he charmed her into believing that he was madly in love with her. Ignoring the ringing bells, Anna thought she had once again found the man she could live with for the rest of her life. In those days, getting a divorce was not easy. The only way a couple could get divorced was if one of the individuals could prove adultery had taken place. After that, they couple would be forced to go through a messy court case. Anna did her part—going through the drama of being the other woman—and it could not have been an easy thing to do. Still, she loved Allan so much and thought she was fighting for the rest of her life.

Allan eventually got his divorce and his freedom—and then told Anna he no longer needed her.

This crushing blow almost put Anna over the edge. Suddenly sinking into a deep depression, she felt her life was over. Anna had been through so much in her life, and when she finally believed that a man was deeply committed to her, she found he had used her to get his divorce. When it was over, he had thrown her out like a dishrag.

So began a desperate time in Anna's life. She could not get herself out of the dark hole she had fallen into. With no end in sight, she did the only thing that she felt she could do: She took a bottle of pills and swallowed them all, hoping she would never awake to another day of pain. However, one of Anna's daughters found Anna, who was unconscious but still breathing. Soon, Anna was rushed to the hospital. After regaining consciousness, and realizing she had survived, Anna was very angry. She had not wanted to be been found in time; she had not wanted to live. For a long time, she couldn't forgive her daughter who had found her and saved her life.

Slowly, Anna recovered and began to rebuild her life. She went back to work once she was well enough, doing whatever jobs she could to keep busy and make money. Using her experiences in both nursing and cooking, she was able to find plenty of work. Not looking for love, Anna went on a few casual dates from time to time, but there was never anything serious. One day, while reading the local newspaper, she found an advertisement for a housekeeper on an island. Her interest piqued enough to enquire more, and eventually go for an interview. Anna learned that the job also entailed helping with five young children between the ages of five and ten. Their mother had walked out on them and their father, Brian.

Anna left the interview, telling herself that there was no way she wanted to accept the job. She didn't have the time or energy to take care of another family. Yet, for some reason, she couldn't stop thinking about the job. Was it the thought of this man struggling to bring up his motherless children? Did she think that the small kids needed a woman in their lives? Whatever the reason was, Anna ultimately decided to take the position of housekeeper for the family on the island.

At that point, Marianne was thirteen years old. She was able to go and live with her older sister and her husband while she completed her education. As Anna set foot on a new path, she embraced Brian's five children as if they were her own. She was no stranger to mothering other people's kids; she had already helped raise four others as well as her own. Over the following months, she really bonded with Brian and his children. They became a family. Eventually, Anna even took Brian's last name. To the outside world, they were just another normal couple, doing their best to raise a family. For a long time, they were truly happy.

As with extended families, though, problems are always bound to come up. This family was no different. As the children became older, they were more aware of the fact that Anna was not their *real* mother. They started to use that against her, reminding her that she was not their real mother; she couldn't tell them what to do. That's when the battles begin.

Furthermore, the children's mother eventually came back into their lives. After that, the problems only became worse. It had been a decade since Anna had made her decision to take on the task of raising those five children. It must have been heartbreaking for her to finally decide she could no longer deal with the constant problems in her life. With that, she packed her things and moved back to Tasmania and into a trailer park.

Anna had always been a very independent person, doing whatever it took to make sure her daughters were taken care of. Now she only had to take care of herself. As the years went by, and her daughters concentrated on their own lives, Anna never asked for help. She felt comfortable simply taking care of herself just as she always had.

We all know—or most of us do, anyway—that as we grow older, we tend to become a little more fragile. That was no different for Anna. Even though she had traveled down many different paths, Anna never forgot where her journey had started or why her life had taken those particular paths. Everything she had gone through was etched in her memory, and it is because of those memories that the last years of her life unfolded the way they did.

Anna began having major problems with one of her legs. Anna's doctor told her that her leg could be operated on; however, there was a slight possibility that the surgery could end up making her leg worse. Anna did not want to lose her leg, and she made that abundantly clear to her family, who know what she had gone through in the past with Gerhard. So it was a traumatic moment when Anna woke up from surgery and was told that the operation hadn't gone as planned. The eighty-three-year-old woman's leg had been amputated.

Anna was livid, feeling that her family had betrayed her. She had been adamant about keeping her leg. With that, she began to freak out, trying to rip the plaster off and throwing whatever she could at the nurses. She could not believe that the one thing she had feared had happened to her. In that moment, she hated everyone—her family most of all. For Anna's family, it had been an incredibly stressful time. They felt they had no other choice in the matter; they didn't want Anna to die on the operating table. While they knew how their mother had always feared the loss of a leg, they loved her and didn't want to say goodbye to her that way.

Anna recovered from her operation and eventually returned home to her small apartment. Even though she had a large and caring family, she wanted to take care of herself. She didn't want to have to rely on anyone else. Living alone in her apartment was comfortable and familiar; it became her way of life. While the building itself looked dingy from the outside, the inside was beautiful. Anna had taken pride in decorating the place to her taste.

Without any savings, Anna lived from paycheck to paycheck, getting by solely on her pension. But at her age, how was she supposed to get around and look after herself with just one leg? Anna's family had gotten her a motorized scooter so that she would be able to get around and still do a lot of the things that she used to do. Having a scooter to get around improved Anna's outlook on life.

One day, there was a knock on Anna's door. Anna opened it to see a salesman standing there. He began telling her all about a wonderful massage chair that could help with her mobility. He told her that it would help her be able to keep her independence. Those were magic words to Anna. Anna also had a credit card. She had made sure to pay her bill each month, never missing a payment, so she had a high credit limit. Well, the salesman made Anna believe that she could easily pay the monthly payment to get the massage chair that would solve all of her problems. With that, she purchased the chair without hesitation.

The massage chair only created more problems, though. Now Anna had to battle with her disability and try and find the extra money out of her small pension to pay off her large credit card balance. Marianne and her family became aware of what had happened and tried to help as much as they could, especially knowing how Anna was not coping very well with the loss of her leg. Marianne also tried to get her mother to make the trip to Australia and live with her and her family in the beautiful home they had made, but Anna refused. Her apartment was her home, and no one was going to persuade her to leave.

As the months went on, and Anna was unable to keep up with her payments, Marianne desperately tried to find a solution for her mother's financial problems. She even approached the bank and tried explaining the situation, noting that the bank should have never have given Anna so much credit in the first place. The bank didn't budge.

Meanwhile, Anna hated feeling helpless and not in control. So when a few young thugs broke into her unit one night, roughing her up while trying to find money that she didn't have, Anna's world came crashing down around her. The only place she knew as home had now been violated; she no longer felt safe. Anna still hadn't fully dealt with the distress of losing her leg, and now she had been violated in the worst possible way—in her own home.

At the same time, the bank became relentless in hassling Anna, looking for the money she had used to pay for the massage chair. The bank hounded her to the point where she began looking for other ways to get money. During the final conversation she had with Marianne, Anna asked her if she could get money from a machine that she had seen on television. Marianne wasn't sure what her mother was referring to; she assumed she had seen an advertisement and was confused. She was feeling desperate and under a lot of stress. She didn't know any better at that point.

Unable to pay back the bank, and suddenly not feeling safe in her home because of the break-in and the attack, Anna saw no way out. To her, there was only one option left: a bottle of pills that sat on the table beside her. She was old and tired and simply wanted peace. She felt her life was shattered. With that, she decided to end it, leaving her family behind to pick up all the pieces.

9. Seeking Help

Since our *Living Beyond Suicide* support group started almost a decade ago, there have been a lot of people who have come to seek help after losing a loved one to suicide. It saddens me to hear about all the lives that have been lost to suicide, knowing how much pain these people are in. Worst of all is the fact that suicide never has to happen. If only the people who had decided to end their lives had reached out and asked for help. *If only.* This is what it always comes down to: *If only we had known how to change what had happened . . .* Sometimes hindsight would be a great help in all of our lives.

When someone chooses to commit suicide, that person's loved ones are suddenly left behind to try and deal with the terrifying realization that they will never see that person again. They are left to cope with the trauma of what never should have happened in the first place. Some people are stunned to hear that a mother—after losing her son twenty years ago— could still be trying to deal with what happened even today. Some people believe that people living in the aftermath of suicide should figure out how to get over it and move on. If you have never been touched by suicide, you will never fully understand; you can only *try* to understand and be supportive.

Speaking from experience with having suicide touch my life— unfortunately, multiple times—I can tell you that it is impossible to just "get over" the fact that a loved one has chosen to take his or her life. However, you *can* gain comfort through sharing experiences or simply telling your story out loud. In time, you can then try to live with what has happened.

One particular woman found out about *Living Beyond Suicide* and decided to attend a session. She realized that in coming to a supportive meeting, she was able to gain a little more understanding. This clarity helped her move on to the next stage of her journey. I also met a man who was desperate to find some kind of comfort after losing his family. He believed his wife died after suffering from a broken heart. The man and his wife had two sons, and one of the sons had died in a car accident. The other son, after not being able to deal with the loss of his brother, decided to commit suicide, which left the parents with a double trauma. That led to the mother losing her will to live, too. I met a couple who had one daughter. At the age of sixteen, she appeared to be happy and healthy. However, after saying goodnight to her parents one evening, she disappeared into her bedroom and took her life. Her family was left devastated with no answers.

The hardest thing for a partner is to know the one he or she loves is in trouble yet not being able to do anything more to help them—or to not even know that there were problems in the first place. I met a man who lost his wife to suicide. She had suffered from depression, leaving him with four very young children. After the loss of his wife, he suddenly had to become both father and mother. For the first time in his life, he really learned what it was to like to be a real parent. While he had been out working all the time, his wife had taken care of their home and family. It all became too much for her. Another young woman, not being able to cope with life anymore, walked out onto a highway and then in front of an oncoming truck. She left behind a husband and a young baby. People have lost partners, sisters, brothers, parents, children, friends—the list just goes on and on.

There are many ways that people have taken their lives, but there is one story that I always think about because it is just so unimaginable. A woman who was also a mother, sister, daughter, and nurse had always suffered from depression. Unfortunately, she endured a lot of pain over the years. One day, just before Christmas, she did a horrific thing: She set herself on fire. It was an act that left her family totally traumatized. It also changed the way the family used to view some of the enjoyments in life, such as holidays, especially for the woman's sister. Now the last thing she ever wants to do each year is put up a Christmas tree and decorations. The memories and the way the young woman chose to die are too traumatic to ever forget.

Over the past years, I have heard of children wanting to die from an early age. That's a hard concept to understand. One would think that a child is far too young to understand death. However, it does happen. It's just that there are so many people in so much pain; age doesn't need to play a factor in it. If only people knew where to go for help, though, or more importantly, know that help is *always* available. They wouldn't have to go through whatever they are going through alone.

Whether a person contemplates committing suicide or not has a lot to do with the serotonin levels in the brain. Serotonin is a hormone in the pineal gland, the digestive tract, the central nervous system, and blood platelets. It plays an important part in the regulation of mood, sleep, learning, and the constriction of blood vessels. Some antidepressant medications affect the action of serotonin.

The first time I heard about the correlation between suicide and serotonin levels was from a doctor who was speaking at a function I attended. The lecture truly helped me understand some of what I could never make sense of. Think of a person who is a diabetic, for example. That person may take special medication or get insulin injections for the rest of his or her life to keep his or her diabetes under control. Well, there are people who need medication to help with their serotonin levels in their brains. The sad thing is, because we cannot physically see there is a problem, it can and does go unnoticed—and then it can be too late for help.

The trouble with mental illness is that it's virtually invisible. You can't get help unless you seek it, or if your doctor or a family member knows there is a problem. If no one knows there's a problem, however, you become a different person to the outside world, just going along with life. In reality, that pain inside is just as bad as physical pain can be. I know this because I have also suffered from a mental illness. It took a long time for me to realize that I needed medication, and even longer to realize that the first medication I was taking was not the right one for me.

Sadly, suicide and the devastating impact it has on others will continue. All we can hope for is the more it is acknowledged and spoken about, the more people will begin to understand that a person does not take his or her own life because he or she wants to. Suicide is an illness. With more understanding, the stigma attached to the word, "suicide," will become less severe. Then, hopefully, the number of suicides each year will be reduced.

There are many places people can go to for help these days much more than a decade ago. Salvation Army have their hope for life programs and by going on line and look for suicide prevention you can also find other avenues.

There is Life Line and there is a twenty four hour number the front of the telephone book has information, other pathways are counselors, health workers Pastoral workers and support services. It is best to look in your own community as they are all different. What works best for us and for others that have fought to have that same model is Standby our Trauma Team, it is twenty four seven as soon as they are notified there has been a suicide and the family would like them in attendance they are there and they are not just there that one time they are there to help you through the most traumatic time of your life, Standby is also linked with ambulance and the police also life line also many more.

10. Support and Awareness

Not long after my only daughter took her life, I was asked to go and speak at a function at Griffith, a rural country town in New South Wales. Looking back, I was probably not the best person to speak because it hadn't been very long since I had lost my third child to suicide. Still, I remember wanting to help and try to stop anyone else from taking his or her life. I thought that if I could help in any way—or even just help save one life—then I needed to go.

What surprised me the most about that community was that the group of people trying to get suicide awareness out there had never been personally affected by suicide before. However, they saw a great need to try and help get awareness out in their community. In doing so, they were helping to save lives. The group was very passionate about the work they were doing, and they were actually making their local government sit up and listen to what was needed within their own community.

The group also made me realize just how little *I* was aware of. I didn't know how serious the problem of suicide really was—and still is, especially in rural areas. I guess it all comes back to the fact that unless you are directly affected by suicide, most people don't want to know. For people who have been traumatized by suicide, however, the pain and confusion ultimately take over your life.

Val Rowe, Ian Carter, and Rev. Louise Osbourne of the Combined Christian Churches banded together with their small team to try and bring suicide prevention to the attention of their whole community. They held all sorts of lectures at various venues to raise money for where it was needed most. At the time I was there, I believe there had been no funding coming from any of the government parties. (One would hope it has certainly changed by now.)

When I got off the bus in Griffith, a small thin woman caught my attention. She sported very short hair with different colors through it. To my surprise, it was Val the woman who had contacted me and asked me to make the trip to Griffith. I quickly learned that what Val lacked in size, she certainly made up for with her heart. One journalist stated in the local newspaper that Val was either "a saint or insane . . . or maybe both" because of her passionate persistence in promoting suicide awareness.

One really great thing the group did was approach the owners of their community swimming pool. There were so many young kids who could not normally afford to go and spend their hot summer days cooling off and enjoying themselves at the pool. The owners gave them a special price, and in doing so, these teenagers had somewhere to go during the summer. Having a fun place to spend time to also helped keep the kids off the streets and out of trouble.

Another of the group's main projects at that time was fighting for beds in their local hospital. Beds weren't available for patients who had gone in after an attempted suicide. For this reason, patients would then be sent home almost as quickly as they arrived. It didn't matter how old the person was or what he or she had done to try and commit suicide. Each patient would be attended to and then simply discharged. (Eventually, the group helped secure a number of beds for attempted suicide patients.)

The few short days I was in Griffith, I became very aware of the many farmers who were committing suicide. This wasn't just in Griffith, but all over the country. So when I finally stood up to speak in front of all those people to tell them my story, I looked out into the crowd and paused for a moment. I knew there would be farmers in that crowd who were struggling to survive. Perhaps, they knew of others who were fighting to keep their farms going. In that moment, I knew I had to say my speech a little differently than I had originally planned.

I had been there to talk about what had happened to my family, and I told my story as openly as I could. I must admit, however, that when I get asked to speak at venues and am told that I only have so many minutes, it does tend to throw me for a loop. I get really nervous! But once I start talking, especially when I'm talking about something that's meaningful and incredibly important to me, I relax a little and do just fine. I remind myself to simply speak from the heart, even if I took the time to carefully write something down. On that particular night, I wanted so much to reach out to the farmers in the room—the ones who had been going through some really bad times. I wanted to try and let them know that if they had to give up their properties or their homes, they would still have something much more important at the end of the day: their families.

People can replace homes and material things; however, lives are irreplaceable. I told the farmers in the audience that just because they were men didn't mean they couldn't hold out a hand and ask for help. I told them to not be afraid to seek help. I pleaded that if they ever even thought about taking their lives, to please don't. Suicide doesn't solve anything, and the trauma the families left behind go through is beyond devastating. Worst of all, the damage done can never be changed. I strongly believe that if my eldest son knew the magnitude of the devastation we have gone through—and will continue to go through for the rest of our lives—I am certain he would have reached out for help, making life so very different.

I like to think I helped some of those people that night. I also believe that suicide awareness is widely spread throughout their community now, thanks to those who cared enough to help those in need and continue to do so. My trip to the little town of Griffith was some time ago now, but one day I would really like to go back.

When you believe somebody is in trouble, and not sure how to help them - all you need to do is let someone know - talk to the family or police, Ring life line. Some of the web sights are:

www.headspace.com

www.sane.org

www.justlook.org.au

www.depresionet.com.au

www.reachout.com.au

www.relationships.com.au

www.beyondblue.org.au

www.kidshelp.com.au

11. The Continuing Ripples

As the days go by, turning into weeks, then months, and finally into years, I often think of a phrase that I heard at one of the many speaking arrangements I have attended. The words go something like this: "When a pebble is dropped into a pond, it sinks to the bottom and out of sight. Yet, it leaves all of these ripple effects behind." Since the deaths of my three children, my life has continued in much of that same way. My children are gone; I will never see them again in this lifetime. However, the ripples that have been left behind by their deaths are constantly flowing on without an end in sight.

There are just so many ripples coming from so many directions. When I lost my youngest brother, Darryl, to suicide, my family's lives changed forever. The trauma his death left us with was so incredibly painful. I remember my kids were all with me at the time of his death, and I still remember the impact it had on them. We openly talked about the way he had died. My kids saw and felt the pain we all went through. We also spoke about his children growing up now without a dad. At the time, they were so very young. Darryl's suicide tore our family apart. It broke up relationships that could never be fixed.

We all had to learn to cope with Darryl's death in the only way we could. There was no help back in those days. Furthermore, there was a huge stigma attached to the word, "suicide." People didn't really hear much about anyone dying that way. They definitely didn't understand it. That haunting question would always come back around: *Why?*

My youngest brother was the first closest person to me to take his life. I still honestly don't believe he meant to do it. However, he had taken pills and he had been drinking a lot, and then he passed out on the floor. Soon after, he became sick and asphyxiated. Either way, the coroner pronounced his death a suicide. We do know that before Darryl took those pills, though, he made a phone call to our older brother, Steven. Unfortunately, the distance was just too far for anyone to get there in time to save his life.

It was a terrible time for all of us, especially my mother. I remember her asking me to stop at the cemetery when leaving the hospital after saying goodbye to her youngest son. When we got there, she got out of the car and lay across my father's grave, sobbing her heart out, wanting my father to comfort her in her loss. My father had only been gone a short time before my brother's death. Darryl was buried on my birthday, the worst birthday I have ever had. He left behind a wife and three young children. Those children were to grow up without their father in their lives.

My own three kids were all home at that time, and they saw the devastation of what their uncle's death did to everyone, including themselves. This is why I know that my eldest son, Terry, the first of my children to take his life, just did not see beyond that narrow, dark tunnel. Otherwise, he would never have followed in his uncle's footsteps. He couldn't have. He would never have wanted to hurt us that way.

Losing Terry totally ripped out my heart. I had never felt such pain before. I remember just wanting to wake up and realize that it was all a horrible nightmare, begging God for it not to be true. I remember the days dragging on in a vague kind of way until Terry's body finally came home. They were days of foggy confusion; I simply could not believe that what had happened was real. I couldn't believe Terry was gone until I actually saw him myself.

When I received the phone call that my son was home, I immediately went to the funeral parlor. On the way over there, I continuously prayed that it was all just an awful mistake. I wanted to be able to walk in and see that somebody else was lying in that coffin. When I entered the room where his body lay, I tried to prepare myself for whatever was to come. But how do you really prepare to see your child lying in a coffin? In some ways, the body *looked* like Terry, but I couldn't touch him. My Terry had been full of life, not an empty shell that only kind of looked like him. Still, I knew that I was gazing down at my son.

When the reality of what was going on finally did start to hit me, one of my biggest concerns was that I would never see Terry again. I was terrified that I would forget his face. I couldn't bear the thought of that. With that, I quickly found every photo I could of him. I even had some of them enlarged just to be sure. Looking back, I now realize that there's no way I could've forgotten my son's face, or the faces of my other two children. Their smiles are etched in my memory forever.

Life would've turned out so differently if Terry had not chosen to commit suicide. Sure, I know there would have been problems to try and deal with; however, I would have much rather have had those issues than attempt to cope with the horror of never seeing him again. Problems can usually be fixed with the right help. Once you are gone, though, it is much too late it. Death is irreversible.

My two sons were very close. Even though there was the normal sibling rivalry every now and then, they got along really well and loved each other. In fact, all three of my children got along; however, the boys had a special bond. After Terry died, it was the start of all those unseen ripples I mentioned—or at least the ones that are unseen by others. I can't say for certain that my second son, Brad, would have not gone down some of the same paths that he did, but I don't believe he would normally have made all those bad choices that led to him also taking his life. Brad's pain and confusion were so traumatic after the loss of his brother that he found a way to deal with the pain: He turned to alcohol and illegal drugs.

With no proper help around at the time, and friends who were only too willing to keep getting drunk and high, Brad's life became a nightmare, not only for himself but also for those who loved him. It is so hard being a parent and seeing your child slowly killing himself, yet knowing you can't do anything about it. Growing up, Brad had a gentle nature. However, in the days before he died, he had become so screwed up and violent that when he was high, I just stayed out of his way. He was so different from the son I once knew and loved.

During those tumultuous years leading up to my youngest son's death, we lived day by day, wondering what was going to happen next. Anyone who says that marijuana does not damage the brain needs a big wakeup call. It *totally* changed my kids' lives, turning them into people I didn't know and, admittedly, didn't like. You may be wondering, *How could she say that, especially since her children are now gone?* Don't get me wrong; *I loved my kids.* However, I will not put them up on a pedestal in trying to say they were such good children or that they did nothing wrong. Smoking marijuana was the start of their downhill paths, and what eventually contributed to them choosing to end their lives.

Brad went from smoking marijuana to stronger substances. One thing is certain: It all started because he could not deal with his brother's suicide. Slowly, his personality changed from that of a gentle boy to one I was afraid of, especially if he was high. I remember how, one day, he picked up his sister and almost put her through a spike on a wooden fence. Luckily, a neighbor intervened and prevented the disaster from happening. Brad also used to try and run in front of traffic and jump off of rooftops. I lost track of how many windows he smashed. One time, he ended up cutting a major artery in his wrist and needed emergency surgery. While Brad was in the hospital, I begged the staff to get help for him, letting them know he was always trying to take his life. All that got me was an even bigger gap in our relationship. The doctors did nothing for my son, and I was a bad mother for saying anything.

Whenever my son came down from his highs, he never remembered the full extent of his actions. He never remembered how violent he had been toward his family. These frightening things happened on such a regular basis that it became totally exhausting to try and deal with. Worst of all, there was nothing we could do. The weeks before Brad took his life, he was feeling incredibly depressed. He felt as if he had lost everything that had been going good for him. For the first time, I believed my son had finally come to realize what his choices were doing to him. I truly thought that he would focus on trying to straighten his life out. He wasn't living with us anymore, however, so I didn't know what was *really* going on.

I always hoped Brad would hit rock bottom one day and suddenly decide to turn his life around. I hoped that if he didn't do it for himself, then he'd at least do it for his own young son, whom he absolutely adored. A few weeks prior to his death, Brad came to the house for a short visit. He took his son with him, along with his on-and-off partner. I had to work for some of their visit, but we did spend time together and had plenty of time to talk and catch up. I sensed that he finally really wanted to try and get his life back on track. We said goodbye that evening, and it was the last time I ever saw my youngest son alive. I had no idea that Brad actually wasn't doing so well.

When a police vehicle pulled into our driveway, I walked to the front door. The moment I heard Brad's name mentioned, I just thought he was in trouble again. But the words that the policeman tried to convey were far different from what I ever expected to hear. He was there to let me know that Brad had taken his life. He had hanged himself. *No way,* I thought. *There's just no way!* Those words were like knives to my heart. I felt like I suddenly had the wind kicked out of me. I doubled up in such intense pain that I couldn't stand up. When the reality of it all finally set in, I just wanted the pain to go away. I wanted to go to sleep and never wake up. It honestly hurt to live.

After hearing the news about Brad, I was in no state to travel down to our home on the south side of Brisbane, which is where my daughter, Tracy, and her family lived. I needed to be with my daughter after what had happened. There were a lot of phone calls made; however, we just didn't connect. Either Tracy was out or John had taken me to see the doctor. I don't remember a lot about that time. All I knew was that I did not want to see my youngest son's lifeless body. I couldn't bear to see *another* son's lifeless body.

The walls in my home back in those days had been covered with pictures of my kids and grandkids, as well as other family members and friends. I remember taking down every photo and placing all of them out of sight. I thought that if I didn't see their faces, I could block out the pain I was feeling. I know now how unrealistic that was. However, I was hurting so badly then that I did not want to think or feel. I stayed in a fog for quite some time. I know I attended Brad's funeral, but I can't really recall any details or memories about it. After the funeral, I became incredibly depressed. I didn't care whether I got out of bed or not. While I did what I needed to do, I was only going through the motions. In the end, I was left with a choice of either getting my life back or ending up in some mental home, not being able to dress myself. I chose to go on living. With that, I started taking medication for my depression. I was determined to have some kind of life.

I believe that things happen for a reason, and I said the same thing in my previous book, *The Healing Beach*. As days went on, I began having nightmares about my sons. I would suddenly wake up and have a full-blown panic attack. These nightmares continued to torment me for a long time. One night, however, as my dream started to turn into that same horrible nightmare, I didn't wake up in a cold sweat. This time, the dream turned into something so totally different. I was sent spiraling inside some kind of tunnel; it was like a powerful force had suddenly picked me up, throwing me weightlessly into the air at an incredible speed. When I finally stopped spinning, I saw both of my sons. Brad was standing on my left. He had the silly smile on his face I always loved to see. Terry was up ahead from us. I remember running toward Terry with tears streaming down my face, crying out, "You're all right! You really are all right!" In that moment, I felt such intense happiness as my eldest son stood there, smiling back at me. When I finally reached Terry, Brad was there beside me again. The three of us just hugged and hugged. I awoke with tears on my face.

If I was ever a skeptic about the afterlife, it ended there. Even though the surreal moment only lasted seconds, I had been able to spend time with my boys again. I knew then that they were together; they were okay. After that night, I stopped having those recurring nightmares. However, a few short months later, I would soon learn that my daughter, Tracy, would also choose to take her life. To this day, I have to wonder if seeing my boys in my dream was God's way of easing the mental trauma I would soon go through because of Tracy's death.

To be honest, I still find it difficult to talk about Tracy at times. My daughter was beautiful and I loved her. Sadly, I know I let her down. After she told me that she was on drugs—just before Brad died—I simply couldn't cope. We had gone through the previous six years watching the way drugs had destroyed Brad's life. I couldn't take any more of it. The day Tracy stood beside her new husband and informed me she was on drugs, I realized that I needed to distance myself from her life, and so I did. It was just too hard to keep going through.

My daughter and I had been close for many years. We had been through so much together. She was the eldest of my three children, and she was the one who had lived at home for the longest. We had our problems, of course, but Tracy always knew her stepfather and I were there for her. However, the loss of Tracy's husband Robert to motor neuron disease— so soon after Terry's suicide—was understandably tough for her. Furthermore, Tracy and Robert had a young son, Bradley, and they had just signed the papers on the loan for their new home the day before Rob's death. I know the hardest thing for her to do was to try and get on with her life.

John and I had bought a home near my daughter, and we tried to help and support her all we could. My biggest mistake, though, with both Tracy and Brad, was handing out money to them whenever they needed it. I didn't realize that all I was doing was giving them the opportunity to use it for things that were not good for them. At the time, I was willing to do anything to try help ease their pain. I thought by giving them money, it would help alleviate the stress of their everyday living, even if it meant that I would be broke.

Tracy never got over Bradley's father, yet she hated to be alone. She tried to find happiness in different relationships that usually ended badly. She began leaning toward men who were completely different from the husband she had once loved. Even though my daughter's life was in turmoil, she was still there beside me through most of the bad experiences we had with Brad. I regret not being there for her during that traumatic time following Brad's suicide.

After all that Tracy had seen and lived through, she still chose to take the same path her two brothers had taken. I found it *incredibly* hard to forgive her for taking her life. My daughter once asked me if I wanted her to be happy. I told her that was what I wanted for her most of all. Tracy never grieved properly for any of her losses; she just tried to get on with life. Unfortunately, her choices were just not right, especially for her. There are those people who have said I interfered too much—and yes, there were times that I did—but I was both a mother and a grandmother. If I believed Tracy was doing the wrong thing, I told her so. Wouldn't any parent? With that said, I would have given anything to make my daughter's life easier, and I did try to do this.

Thinking back to Tracy's younger years, I have tried to remember where her lack of pride and self-esteem came from. She had been beautiful, both inside and out. As children, my kids were always dressed decently, never having to depend on hand-me-downs. Still, from the time Tracy started choosing her own clothes, she dressed in outfits that were much too big for her, especially her tops. She had long dark hair, which was always hanging loosely around her face. Very rarely did she ever wear makeup. To this day, I wonder, *Was it because she never had a doting father?*

Fathers and daughters often form a close bond that generally starts from the time the baby is born. However, Tracy never had that experience with her dad. I don't ever recall her father sitting her on his lap and telling her she was his princess. He never told her that he loved her more than anything in the world. I have asked myself so many times if my daughter paid the high price for my mistakes. I so wish I could go back and change things for her and my two sons, but I can't. All I can do now is try to be there for my grandchildren.

Eventually, I realized that I had been suffering with depression through my children's growing-up years. Being aware of that has helped me to understand a lot of the choices I made, as well as the unfortunate things that happened because of this. I do know that I did the best I could under the circumstances, and I did love my three kids more than anything in the world. It was because of them—and the damage done to them by their father and me—that I did break up the family unit. Unfortunately, I should have taken those permanent steps years before. This is one of my biggest regrets; however, I can't go back and change my life. I must continue to live with those decisions I made at the time.

I know what it is like to have been on the edge. I know what it is like to be so down that you really believe that you think that everyone would be better off without you. At the time, all you can see is that the pain of living is just too much to handle; there is no way out. I found out, though, that life *is* worth living. No matter what happens, it is good to be alive. Even if you are suffering, there are ways you can be happy and also have a life.

Suicide. It is just one word, but if spoken, it says it all: Somebody has taken his or her life. It is a word that is not used much unless it has directly touched our lives. Why? Is it because of the stigma that is still attached to it or maybe because the thought of it creates fear. There is also the total lack of understanding about suicide. It is hard to understand why people choose to end their lives.

Over the years, there have been times when I have brought up the fact that I lost my youngest brother and my three children to suicide. I'm never surprised to receive different kinds of reactions. Usually, after the initial shock fades, I get an "Oh, you poor thing!" type of response. Someone else once said, "Gee, you don't look like you have any pain in your face!" (Admittedly, that was a hard one to hear.) Then there are people who know what has happened, and they keep their distance for their own reasons.

I suppose I don't really need to tell others that I lost my children to suicide; however, that is what happened. Terry, Brad, and Tracy were my kids, and I should be able to talk about them if I want to. After all, they were a big part of my life and always will be. It doesn't matter that they are no longer on this earth. My children's actions created ripples in my life and in the lives of those who loved them. Those ripples will never go away.

Over the years, there have been times when I have beaten myself up, feeling like I must have been the most awful mother to have lost all of my children. I should have been able to save them. But with the help of our group support and the wonderful people I have met through the Standby team, I have come to understand so much. Without the help and support I received, I don't believe I would have been able to live a quality life with happiness ever again. I was never supposed to have lost my kids first. No parent should have to go through that trauma of burying their children. Do I still blame myself? I definitely take some of the responsibility. However, my kids had their own journeys to travel, and it was *their choices* that ultimately led to their deaths.

We can always go back in hindsight, but would it *really* have made a difference? That is something I don't think anyone can answer. At the end of the day, we are not responsible for someone else choosing to take his or her life. After Terry died, I always believed that if he knew the ripple effect his suicide created, he would never have taken his life. One of the hardest things for me to live with is that my other two kids, Brad and Tracy, had lived through the trauma and devastation of losing Terry to suicide—and yet they made that same choice. For me, it was so hard to help my children, especially since Brad and Tracy were young adults and had other outside influences in their lives. There wasn't any professional help back in those days; suicide was still very much taboo. There was just nowhere to go.

Looking back, I don't know if the things I wish I had changed would have made any difference; I will never know. I do believe, however, that I did the best I could at the time. I know I loved my kids very much, and even though there were times that I hated what they did with their lives, I still loved them unconditionally. I did not know much about depression in those days either or that it was a condition I suffered from. Sometimes I wonder how life would have been if I had been given the right medication. Would I have been able to change some of the things that had taken place in our lives? Those six years between when I lost Terry, and then Brad, were the worst times in all my life. I felt so powerless, trying to get doctors to understand that Brad was not just suffering from substance abuse; he just never coped with his older brother's death.

Unless you are a parent who has been through what I have been through, you will probably never fully understand. You see your child slipping away from you, and you know your child is taking substances that he or she shouldn't be taking. However, there is nothing you can do because you are only a parent. Ultimately, kids will do what kids want to do. Furthermore, once they turn eighteen years old, suddenly you have no rights. Your children suddenly have the right to decide their own destinations, even if that means making wrong choices. Now I am not talking about the choices of they want to make career-wise or anything like that. I'm talking about when you can see that your child is slowly killing himself or herself by destroying his or her body. You know your child isn't thinking straight. It is such an exhausting feeling because you don't know where to go next for help. You don't know what to do to make things right. It was just so hard for me.

Do I believe my kids suffered from depression? I'm not entirely sure. However, I do believe that Terry suffered from depression, and I still believe—given the right support at the right time—it would have made all the difference in the world if he had been able to receive the help he needed. His death changed all of my family's lives. Unfortunately, the ripples he left continued into Tracy and Brad's lives, too, as well as into the lives of their children and everyone who knew and loved him.

These days, I find myself putting on smiles for all to see. However, even after all these years, it is still a battle at times. I try to stay positive, mostly because of those still-continuing ripples that have been caused through the deaths of my children. I have learned to live without my kids, but they are always with me in my heart. I miss them terribly every day. It is not just the loss of my children; it has been the loss of being a part of my grandchildren's lives. It's heart-wrenching to see them torn away from each other, never being allowed to even visit because of the court system.

I realize that we are not the only grandparents who have been cut off from seeing their grandchildren. There are also those who don't see theirs because of broken relationships or maybe because of a family death. Perhaps, the parents have just cut the grandparents out of their lives. There are many different reasons, and it is sad because the grandchildren are the ones who ultimately miss out. We can never get back the years that go by.

We have had our grandson, Bradley, since he was just twelve years old. I refused to send him back to where the courts had originally placed him. When I decided to walk away from the court case, and the battle of trying to keep my two eldest grandchildren together, I knew that I had tried my best with what I was able to do at the time. With our finances being as they were, it was what I knew I had to do. John and I both love Bradley and Emma as we do our other grandchildren, yet with the Australian court system, even though we are only in another state, we may as well be in a different country. We did what we had to and tried to get on with our lives.

During the months following Tracy's death, there were many times when my ex-husband would call me, obviously drunk, and say that Bradley needed to be with John and me. As always, I told him that Bradley was always welcome; he could send him to us whenever he wanted to. With that, flights were booked and plans would be put into place. But by morning, once my ex-husband was sober again, I'd be told that our grandson wasn't coming—or I wasn't told at all.

I made a vow after yet another flight that had to be canceled that when John and I did get the opportunity to get our grandson up to where we lived, he was not going back. While the courts had put Bradley where they thought he would be best cared for, the courts were also told a bunch of lies by people who had their own agenda to stop the kids from coming to us. Meanwhile, I was in the Queensland hospital; it was the afternoon of my daughter's funeral.

My eldest grandson did finally get sent up to us. When we realized it was definitely going to happen, I was happy that I would get the chance to try and give Bradley the life that he deserved. It wasn't fair that he had gone through so much tragedy at his young age. In fact, it hadn't been fair for any of the grandchildren.

When John and I went to meet our grandson at the Brisbane Airport, Bradley had just barely turned twelve years old. The first thing I noticed about Bradley was that even though he had grown, he was *so* skinny. His arms were so thin that I almost could've surrounded the top half of his arm with my thumb and forefinger. Additionally, his demeanor had changed. The young boy who used to be so excited to see us was shy and withdrawn. I knew that it had been a long time since he had been given any affection.

I didn't expect Bradley to be the same young boy I had last seen, but there had been such a huge change in him. By his actions alone, I could tell that there was a lot of emotional trauma locked up inside of him that had never been dealt with. He also had visible health and hygiene issues, and his hands shook when he put his arms out. John and I were truly shocked at the physical and emotional change in the young boy. To be honest, even though we had no idea what we would be in for, I did not expect to find Bradley in the condition he was in.

The poor child's first trauma was the loss of his father before his second birthday. Even though he would not have understood what had happened, he saw his mother in tears often. He knew that something was wrong even if he didn't fully understand. Over the years, Bradley also went through the emotional upsets and changes his mother suffered with the different partners she was with. Then there were the drugs, the abuse, and eventually the suicide of his uncle. Bradley was only ten when my daughter Tracy died. At the same time, he had the one sister who had grown up with him ripped away from him.

It was just before Christmas when Bradley came to us. As soon as I saw him, I knew that John and I would need help. We would never be able to help Bradley on our own. Fortunately, because of my contacts through the support groups, we were able to start getting Bradley the attention and care that he desperately needed. We were never sure if he had ever had any professional help in dealing with the trauma he had lived through; however, we knew that he needed to talk to someone quickly.

When a child is clearly dealing with a lot, it can be so hard to know exactly how to help. I knew Bradley better than anyone, though, and I knew I was not sending him back to where he came from. Schooling became another issue. One reason the courts made the decision to leave our grandson in New South Wales was because he was going to a special class for his learning difficulties. The special class that he had been attending was a class consisting of children with Down syndrome, among other disabilities. I strongly believed he shouldn't have been there. In fact, I had spent many times with my two eldest grandchildren, and was there for those first three years that Bradley attended school.

When John and I approached the principal of our local public school to enroll our grandson, I explained to him that I did not have any previous records for him. I also told him that I did not have Bradley legally and explained why. I also let him know that Bradley was not going back to New South Wales no matter what. It was decided that Bradley would go into the class he was supposed to be in for his age. He would also be properly assessed. Bradley stayed in that class; however, he did receive a lot of extra help and support. With the extra attention, he began to do wonderfully well!

John and I can't take all the credit for helping Bradley to become the young man he has become. Aside from the professional help he received, we were lucky enough to have good friends surrounding us. Our friends were there for us no matter what, helping us through some pretty tough times. Our neighbors, Steve and Shana, and their young daughter, who was around the same age as Emma, were amazing support. Steve and Shana's two older boys were also a good influence in our grandson's life.

Bradley spent a lot of time with Steve and Shana's family during those first years he lived with us. In fact, Steve took him under his wing, trying to teach him things he had never learned before. Steve became a positive male figure in Bradley's life, and his family unit became a surrogate, in a way, for the one that my grandson had missed out on. Steve and Shana included Bradley in their family outings, and they were there for our family many times. For example, there was a time when Bradley went missing from his class one day. I immediately called Steve to say he was missing, and he immediately jumped into his car and started driving around in the pouring rain while I went searching in another direction. Additionally, it was never any trouble if I landed on their doorstep, day or night, just needing some advice or to let off steam.

Even though the courts had advised that Bradley and Emma see each other, it never happened. When Bradley was about to turn fourteen, we traveled the four hours to where we knew Emma attended school, knowing we only had one chance to let them see each other. When our granddaughter came to the office, she didn't even recognize her brother at first. However, when they realized they were being reunited, their young faces just totally lit up. Our granddaughter was so happy to see us! She was allowed to spend the whole lunch break with her brother. Unfortunately, that was the last time the kids saw each other. While John and I did try to get Emma's father to allow the kids to visit each other again, he wouldn't allow it. In fact, we'd show up at his house and he wouldn't even come to the door. It was frustrating, especially for Bradley, but there was nothing more we could do.

12. Where Are They Now?

Janine and Ron are still very much involved in helping others who have lost someone to suicide. We still hold our support group meetings at their home; however, they have moved on in their everyday lives, trying to focus on the good things life has to offer. They spend a lot of time with their family. In fact, their daughter, Renee, now has three beautiful children of her own. Additionally, Janine and Ron see Harley's only son on a regular basis. They have learned to find comfort and happiness from the growing family that surrounds them. The loss of Harley continues to leave a big gap in their lives that will never be filled, and they don't even try to fill it. Harley is and always will be in their hearts.

There were some big changes in Barbara's life after the loss of her daughter, Dianna. Barbara continued to come to group meetings every now and then for the first couple of years; however, once she found out she was going to become a grandmother, she realized it was time to start focusing on the positive things in life. I think this was a good thing for her health and overall wellbeing. After the birth of her grandson, who had become the center of her life, Barbara immersed herself in concentrating on her family around her.

Pauline has moved on with her life in a positive way. She is happy being a grandmother. We don't get to see much of her these days because of her work commitments, but she is still a part of our group whenever possible. She also still comes to different functions when she can.

Sammy appears to be happy. She has a gorgeous little girl and recently gave birth to a baby boy, and she says that she absolutely loves being a mother. She admits that the impact of her father's suicide has been hard for her to deal with, even years later. Sammy still helps out with young people when needed, knowing just how important it is to have that support and having somebody to talk to.

Cassie has been doing exceptionally well. She traveled overseas on a working holiday for a couple of years and is now living in New Zealand with her partner. Cassie is expecting her first child, and she and her partner recently bought their first home. Cassie is such a different young woman from the young girl I first met. I know it has a lot to do with the help she received and the active role she played in starting Head High.

William is happy. He works and lives in Brisbane, and he also still volunteers his time with Head High when needed. Over the years, he has been asked to stand up and speak in front of young kids about the impacts of suicide. It is because William himself received help and support that he has been able to reach out to other children in a positive way.

I know there are times when the family still has bad days; Ken left a big hole in their lives. Still, that doesn't mean they can't be happy. Being involved with our support groups and being there for others, in general, has helped Pauline, Sammy, Cassie, and William move forward with their lives.

Unfortunately, I'm not really sure how Jenny is doing these days. The last I saw her was maybe three or four years ago when I went to a café to have coffee with my sister. Jenny was actually working there. I was happy to see her, and she came over to greet me. After giving me a hug, she told me she that she was doing okay. My grandson used to see her occasionally, but hasn't for a while now. I am just glad that she was working and staying busy. She has so much more life to live.

Marianne will always regret that she couldn't get her mother to make the move to live the rest of her days with her. It was so painful to watch the mother she loved slip further into depression because of her health. Unfortunately, because of the distance, Marianne was not able to see her mother on a regular basis. After her mother died, Marianne came to our group meetings, hoping to gain some kind of understanding in how to live with what had happened. As with most people who are impacted by suicide, it is always the "what ifs" that haunt the mind; so many questions are left unanswered. The last time I saw Marianne, though, she was well and living life one day at a time.

These days, Bradley is doing well. Admittedly, it has been hard raising him at times, but it is a small price to pay to see him make something of his life and have some kind of happiness. As for my other grandchildren, Brad's son contacted me a couple of years ago, and we have spent some time together. It really stunned me when I saw him for the first time after so many years. He looked so much like his dad. In recent months, I saw some words my grandson had written on Facebook: ALL I WANT IN THE WHOLE WORLD IS MY DAD. Those words tugged at my heartstrings, especially since I know how much his dad loved him.

Emma came into our lives right before Christmas. She was just about to turn sixteen. She is a pretty young girl and she knows it. In fact, she's very different from the little girl we used to know. One day, she gave us a little insight into what her life had been like growing up with her father. I don't believe everything that kids tell me; however, I do know some of the history. Emma's paternal grandmother kept a diary and Emma tore a page out of it when she gave it to me to read, it was exactly what we had tried to tell the courts, Emma's father was violent. At the time of my daughter's death he was homeless; he only wanted his daughter for money and it also had accounts of his instability. Emma told us that she had gone to live with her other grandmother for a while before going back, once again, to live with her father.

Emma's life has been pretty much as we predicted it would be. We know nothing can make up for those years she and her brother, Bradley, grew up never seeing each other. Later, I learned that Emma was told we never wanted anything to do with her. How dreadful people are to want the power of control so much that they don't stop and think about the kids and what is best for them! Bradley and Emma went through years wishing that they had each other, and they should never have been separated. The bond between them was broken, and while they can try to repair it, it will never be the same.

There is still so much outside interference where our grandchildren are concerned. However, I learned long ago to step back. The kids now have their own journeys to travel. I recently told Bradley that our roles as parents are pretty much over. We tried to teach him all we could. Now I would like to just be a grandmother. That role was taken away from us, and we had to be the parents our grandson didn't have. I must admit that I hated that because it was hard not being able to spoil him as normal grandparents do with their grandkids. The only extra money we got from the government was twenty dollars a week, and that was because Bradley was an orphan. I wish we could've been more financially able to do what we would have liked to.

It is because of raising Bradley that John and I joined a group called Grandparents As Parents (GAP). This group has grown so much over the years, and it is a great support system for people finding themselves raising their grandchildren like their own children. GAP is a part of Community Solutions, located on the Sunshine Coast, and the employees are very passionate about trying to help struggling grandparents in organizing different activities each month for the families. The program also gives kids a chance to get together with each other, and in doing so, it helps kids realize that they are not alone.

Young kids growing up in today's world are so different from our times, and even my own children's era. First, there is the lack of freedom because of safety issues. In most families, where both parents work, the parents tend to give their kids all the latest electronics, which leads to children staying at home, glued to their video games, or staring down at their smartphones all day long. Kids are becoming antisocial and overweight during the best years of their lives, thanks to the parents who enable them to do so. Then there are the non-working parents who simply do not want to work. They don't mind living off the state if they can. In living this way, they are teaching their kids the same way of life. Let's not forget the kids who have drugs or violence in their lives, and the kids living with a parent who suffers from a mental illness.

There are extended families where kids are shuffled between parents, having to adjust to different sets of rules and sharing with the kids of the other partners. At times, they must feel that they don't belong anywhere. What sort of a secure routine do these kids have? Isn't stability and familiarity what we believe kids need? I watched a segment on television once where families and children from broken homes were being interviewed. I remember thinking about the people who had been selected for the interview. They were probably middle- to upper-class families. It made me wonder about lower-class families in the real world, and how constant shuffling can negatively impact kids.

My journey has shown me so much about life that I never knew. It has opened my eyes to the many children who are suffering from living in homes where a parent has a mental illness. I once volunteered my time at a camp, which is a part of Youth Mental Health Service, called Sunshine Coast Koping Network. I became involved because Bradley needed support when he first came to live with us. Our grandson took part in the organization's Middle Earth program, and then went to the camp I volunteered to help at later on. Andrew and Sharon, with the help of others, run this camp every year for kids who are in need of a break from their everyday lives. At the same time, they get to learn about and work on problem-solving, individual coping strategies, communication skills, emotional identification, relationship maintenance, mental illness awareness, and understanding education.

The camp only ran for four days, but it went from early morning until nighttime. The kids were split into groups where they competed against each other in various activities, including canoeing, wall climbing, swimming, treasure hunts, and crafts. After arriving the first day, the children were sent to find their rooms. I happened to come across a couple of young girls in their early teens. They were proudly showing off the scars they had from cutting themselves. I was so shocked that I was speechless. During those four days, I quickly learned just how much kids are affected by the environments they're put in. It's usually worse when a parent has a mental illness. It was heartbreaking to see how troubled most of the kids were because of what life dealt them. It definitely opened my eyes a bit wider. Unfortunately, the camp only happens once a year. The organization can only accept a small group of kids due to lack of funding. I hope that changes someday.

Even though there are so many people in the world who need support of some kind, I have certainly not gone without needing it myself. While moving into a new house one day, I injured my back pretty badly, which required back surgery. For the next years, I went through some pretty low times. It was frustrating for me not being able to do normal everyday activities. However, my family and friends were there for me, and so were a couple of people from our support group. While I was recuperating, I found myself missing my kids terribly, especially my daughter. I began to pity myself, wondering how life could be so unfair. I know I had far too much time to dwell on my life and what had happened over the years. Either way, it was a pretty depressing time for me. In the end, though, I managed to get through it.

I try to look for something positive to focus on. As cliché as it may sound, I've noticed that when one door closes, another door really does open. Admittedly, life is certainly very different from how I envisioned it would be for myself. I have tried to wander off and try something new with my life, but my focus has always been on trying to help support others—especially those who have lost a loved one to suicide. That's what I always go back to.

I know there are many kids out there who need support. Even though we were able to organize our Head High group, it is not actively running today. The main reason for this is due to lack of funding. Our young people's group was very successful and helped a lot of kids, though. In the future, I would love to see a drop-in center for kids under the age of eighteen. I believe once-a-month meetings aren't enough for kids, and they tend to steer away from doctors and professional counselors. If they had a place to go whenever they really needed to talk to somebody, I think it would save a lot of troubled kids. Let's face it: It would also save the government a lot of money, too, because the kids would get the help they need before they start having major issues in their lives.

I don't have all the answers yet, but I do know if the center were a comfortable and safe place that was managed by young adults who went through similar experiences, kids would be able to identify with these young adults. That's a huge first step in gaining trust, which leads to opening up and beginning the healing process. Obviously, there would need to be guidelines set in place and professionals working with the kids, too. Just being involved in the Head High group showed that a program like this really works. Kids need a place they can go. A support group is long overdue, and it would save a lot of our young kids from going down potentially bad paths. It would also help alleviate some of the negative ripples I've been talking about.

As a parent or caregiver of a child, we think we know our kids and what is going on in their lives; but do we *really?* After losing someone to suicide, adults can get so caught up in their own pain and confusion that they forget about how everyone else is coping, especially children. Unfortunately, a lot of kids won't talk to their parents about how they really feel for various reasons. They bottle up their emotions, and then eventually they act out because the pain becomes too unbearable. It is those actions that can ultimately decide their fate.

After losing somebody that you love, especially before that person is supposed to die, your whole outlook on life changes. When it is a loss by suicide, the trauma of knowing your loved one is gone—that the person *chose* to die—is incredibly overwhelming. As the shock starts to subside, then the indescribable pain begins to hit you—the reality that you cannot go back and change what has happened. You may feel a deep sense of betrayal because the person you loved did not feel like he or she could come to you for help. There are so many different stages and emotions you go through when dealing with the ripples of suicide, and it's important to realize that we don't all grieve the same way. We may deal with our loss differently than another person, and that is okay.

It is important to seek help if you need it. Getting help really *will* change how you live out the rest of your life. Through my own experience, and after hearing what others have had to say, the more we talk about our feelings and what has happened in our lives, the faster we can begin the healing process. I must stress, though, that while help and support can come from family or close friends, it is extremely important to receive help from specially trained professionals. If you don't seek professional help, it could be detrimental to your recovery. There are many people who think they can deal with their pain themselves; they don't want to ask for help. Some try drowning their sorrows, shutting out the world, and then maybe moving on to drugs or alcohol. Eventually, these temporary fixes will take over their lives, and they will believe that there is nobody out there to help. Don't let it get to that point.

There is help out in our communities now far more than there ever was a decade ago. By educating ourselves to look for signs in our friends and family members, and by learning more about suicide prevention, we can hopefully save somebody from taking his or her life. You may think suicide will never touch you, and I hope it never does, but there are more people who die from suicide than in car accidents each year. While you will eventually learn to live with your loss, it will stay with you every day of your life.

I believe that *everybody* needs somebody at some point in his or her life. You can't deal with your pain and stress alone. If you have been affected by someone who chose to commit suicide, or if you are considering taking your life, you need to take advantage of what has been put in place in our communities. Getting help can have a very real impact on how your journey continues. I sincerely hope that you *want* it to continue, especially after reading these personal stories. Remember: The ripples of suicide are continuous, and life is just too precious to waste.